Womanpriest

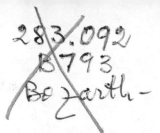

Womanpriest

A Personal Odyssey

ALLA BOZARTH-CAMPBELL

PAULIST PRESS
New York/Ramsey, N.J./Toronto

Acknowledgements

Some of the poems in this book have been published elsewhere:

"Rapport," in THE LIVING CHURCH (Vol. 153, no. 10, Sept. 4, 1966); "New Apostles, New Wine," in THE WOMAN (Sept., 1975); "Talitha Cumi," in CONTEMPLATIVE REVIEW (Vol. 9, no. 3, Summer, 1976); "Call," in IN GOD'S IMAGE: TOWARD WHOLENESS FOR WOMEN AND MEN (New York: Division for Mission in North America, Lutheran Church in America), 1976, and in ENERGY OF MIRACLES: PAINT-INGS BY JULIA BARKLEY (Minneapolis: Daily Press), 1977; "Lovesong in the House of Quarrelsome Overseers," in THE WITNESS (Oct., 1976); "God Is A Verb," in THE ENERGY OF MIRACLES, in PLUMBLINE (Vol. 4,. no. 1, June, 1976), and in CHANNEL (Vol. 20, no. 2, Spring, 1977); "Creation" and "Incarnation," in CHANNEL (same issue); "The Tao of Physics," and "Universal Body," also in CHANNEL; "Mother Christ, Sister Spirit," in PLUMBLINE (same issue as above), CHANNEL, and ENERGY OF MIRACLES; and "Bakerwoman God," in IN GOD'S IMAGE and CONTEMPLATIVE REVIEW (Vol. 9, no. 2, Spring, 1976).

Definitions for Psychic Survival were printed in similar form as "Sister Alla's Survival Kit," in the May-June-July, 1976 issue of *de-liberation*.

The chapter entitled "God Is A Verb" was published in slightly different form in CHANNEL, Volume 20, number 2, Spring, 1977.

I extend my deepest thanks to Phil Bozarth-Campbell and Meredith Montgomery, who helped by reading the manuscript, asking it excellent questions, and checking for errors. My thanks to them for encouraging me through the difficult process of gathering events and thoughts into form.

Cover design by Spencer Drate.
Cover photo by William D. Pletsch Jr.

Library of Congress
Catalog Card Number: 78-58957

ISBN: 0-8091-0243-9

Published by Paulist Press
Editorial Office: 1865 Broadway, New York, N.Y. 10023
Business Office: 545 Island Road, Ramsey, N.J. 07446

Printed and bound in the
United States of America

SN. 9,95 /5,10 /6/30/81

Contents

Introduction	vii
Present	1
Parents	13
Friends	27
Teachers	39
Sisters	46
Ecumenical Oblates	56
Diaconate	77
Marriage	89
Priesthood Frustrated	101
Priesthood Fulfilled	113
Controversy	144
Christian Feminism	166
We Are The Church	177
God Is A Verb	198
Possibility	219

This book is dedicated
to the cowering hero
in all of us

Introduction

It has occurred to me that in reading this book, you will be spending a part of your life with me as I am with you in writing it. I'm aware that you and I are forming a kind of relationship despite the obvious hindrances of space and time. You are at this very moment (which is *your* moment, not mine) speaking my written words inside your own body, making them come alive within you, re-sounding them inside yourself. This is how you meet me, hearing my words resonating with the language of your own reality, reverberating within the clarifying framework of your own experience. I begin and you complete our meeting in this very spirited, very physical way. We begin to stretch out toward one another.

I don't want this book to be a mere monologue frozen in print, a one-way communique, though it's true that a book is a kind of frozen dialogue in the same way that a photograph is. The person who looks at the image in the photograph or hears the speaker in a book can't be seen or heard in return. This is the reader's protection, but also the reader's isolation. Yet, I know that your receptivity is a gift to me, just as my re-presentation in print is an offering to you. I'm offering you at best a partial picture, but a speaking picture, not a mute snapshot. For both of us in different ways, this meeting is at the same time a condensation, a limitation, and an expansion of ourselves, and though we can finally only imagine one another, we are in some real way together.

I once heard a story about a great spiritual teacher. Her own teacher was a Sufi master. When she was his disciple and still quite young, he told her that when she herself became a master she must never teach anyone what she herself had not experienced. I am not here to teach you but to tell you a story and to show you my own process of growth and change and reflection through that story. Taking the old master's wisdom to heart, I can share with you only what I myself have come to know through experience.

I have many questions, many reflections, some contradictions, frequent inconsistencies. Sometimes I have a clear observation, and perhaps too often I have a strong opinion. I invite you to lay out your own questions beside mine, to bounce your reflections off mine, to think about your own observations, explore your own contradictions, examine your inconsistencies, and to challenge my occasional strong opinions.

The only truth I have to tell here is my own, and I'm eager for the process. I believe it will be a whole-making and revealing one for me, and I wish the same for you as you bring your own processes to meet mine.

I can't resist this afterword about the way the book itself came to be. Today while I sat down to the task of typing the last draft for my publisher, having finished the above introduction, I put a clean piece of paper in the typewriter for Chapter One. Now it's a lavish, green spring day, warm, alive with grass and lilac smells making my nose drunk as they come in through my open window. The radio is playing, though I'm not paying much attention to it. Just as I was about to type out the first sentence, "I'm dancing," the music in the room entered my consciousness. A song I love: "I Can See Clearly Now, the Rain Is Gone," and I just *had* to get up and *dance*. My friend Heather was sitting on the purple rug in my study, diligently pouring over and organizing my dishevelled files on recent Episcopal church history, gleaning relevant data for her doctoral dissertation.

"Heather," I said, "look, I really am dancing, just as I'm about to write out the words! This is wonderful. I really *do* write organically; everything in life really *is* connected!" Not that I ever doubted it, but it's a message that springs up so constantly and so unexpectedly and with such delight that I can't help but act amazed every time it happens. Beginning this book again—for the last time—helps me recognize all the connections, to see them more clearly, celebrate them, live them, love them. Alleluia!

Present

I'm dancing. The last Sunday in January. Noon. Colored light dancing in through the long colored windows. And I'm dancing. I'm dancing in this holy space, in this place where people worship, in this church. I'm your priest, God, and I'm offering this dance to you.

It's been a long three years since my ordination to the priesthood. I've changed, grown, gone through moments I thought I couldn't survive for the pain, and moments I thought I couldn't survive for the joy. This moment is one of the joyful ones. My whole being is bursting with gratitude.

You, God, have brought us to this moment, battleworn and scarred, but whole, better, richer, even happier for having gone through it in just the hard way we did. After such a long time of pain and frustration and despair and real danger, Phil and I are finally able to witness to your priesthood publicly together, expressing our priesthood in the community among others as we have privately in our marriage with each other. For this moment, God, I thank you.

Earlier this month, on the Feast of the Epiphany, the Bishop of the Episcopal Diocese of Minnesota publicly recognized the priesthood of the two women priests in Minnesota—Jeannette Piccard and myself—after our long engagement with him to do so since our controversial ordina-

1

tions in Philadelphia with nine other women in 1974. A few days later, Phil asked me to preach in his parish and concelebrate the Eucharist with him this Sunday morning. I was happy to accept the invitation.

On the afternoon a few weeks before the service when I attended to the scripture readings for that particular Sunday, I discovered that the Old Testament reading was to be from the first chapter of Jeremiah. "Phil!" I called out to my spouse in another room, "I can't do this! Look, this reading is the very same passage that gave me the courage to go to Philadelphia to be ordained three years ago. How can I preach on it and not bring in my own experience?" (It had always been my policy not to intrude my personal agenda upon the integrated themes of liturgical readings.)

"You're looking at the old lectionary," Phil answered. "At St. George's we use the lectionary in the 'Blue Book.' " Much relieved, I lay aside my old "Green Book" and consulted the "Blue Book." It was probably the only day in the liturgical year when the two books agreed on the scripture readings. "What shall I do now?" I asked. Phil shook his head and laughed at me and said, "I guess this once you're just meant to share your personal experience in your sermon."

"Before I formed you in the womb, I knew you. Before you came to birth I consecrated you. I have appointed you to be a prophet to the nations." So begins God's call to Jeremiah. And then, this great prophet of Israel, Jeremiah, talks back: "*Oy vey*, God, did you make a mistake!" (My loose translation.) "Listen, I'm much too young for this. I'm just a kid. Please, go find somebody else." Three years ago nothing gave me greater courage than being reminded that even that great prophet Jeremiah was scared to death when he received a challenge to do something rather risky and demanding for God. If *he* tried to get out of *his* important job, I shouldn't feel too badly about my own cowardice in this relatively small thing God was asking of me. "Go to Philadelphia to be or-

2

dained a priest by a retired bishop without my own bishop's consent, without the concurrence of the Episcopal Church let alone all of Christendom? Risk my whole ministry just to claim your gift to me of priesthood? Expose myself and my sister priests to an uncertain future in the Church? You've got to be kidding, God! Listen, I'm only a woman. Please, go find somebody else to try to open up your full ministry to women. I can't be responsible for helping to create a whole priesthood." If God didn't let Jeremiah cop out on the large task of calling back the People of Israel to righteous ways, God certainly wasn't going to let me get away with it in the smaller task of stirring things up a bit in the Episcopal Church. I went to Philadelphia. Before, during, and long after that memorable July 29th, I and my sister priests were held up constantly by the loving and supportive arms of those in the Christian community and beyond it who believed, sometimes more than we, that our irregular ordinations were a good and necessary thing for the whole Church.

I decided to take the opportunity, this Sunday morning, to witness to the prophetic calling of all of God's people. Each one of us is called by God to be something unique in the universe. Your life and mine is the unfolding discovery of what that means for each of us.

As each of us lays claim on our calling, on the particular way of becoming a whole person whose life has meaning for ourselves and for others, we both receive the unique gift from God that is our life, and give back to the universe the varied gifts of our existence. When we do this together, bringing our search, our longings, our discoveries to each other, we create community. And as a community, when we keep our focus God-centered, we're able to speak to the world from the reality of our relationship with God. This is what it means to serve the world in God's name, to be a prophetic people. The age of the solo prophet has given way to the age of genuine community, and if prophecy—speaking

3

in God's behalf—is to take place, it takes place with all of us acting together in God's name and out of love for the whole world, not in general, but in particular. That was my message that morning to the people of St. George's. I affirmed their ministry together as a caring community, a ministry that I have personally experienced through the warmth of individuals who have expressed their Christ-like caring to me in a personal way. I affirm each person in her or his becoming. I affirm all communities formed out of genuine engagement with the Gospel and genuine care for our human family and the whole creature world. I thank everyone who has enriched my priestly ministry by the expression of the priesthood we all share together.

And this brings me to another affirmation, another word of gratitude that for me is most important. As I told the people of St. George's: "I affirm and celebrate publicly today not only my own priesthood, but the priesthood and personhood of your rector, my spouse, who is not only my companion in life, but my colleague in the priesthood, and my brother in Christ." More than anything, God, I was grateful for the opportunity of saying these words publicly. You alone know their full meaning, the incredible growing, struggling, and healing from which they come.

It's amazing, the way in which Phil and I have discovered our very different styles of ministry. It delights me to see him in his own community. He works well within the parish structure, and he enjoys it. He enjoys working with groups, the whole social, people-oriented side of parish life. And because he enjoys himself in ministry, his congregation enjoys him. He and they know how lucky they are to have each other.

And I'm also blessed by my own peripheral contact with this parish. It would be so easy for people to identify my ministry with Phil's, but this doesn't happen. I know, on those special occasions when I visit St. George's, that the warm welcome I receive isn't just because I'm married to the

4

rector, but because of who I am as a person and as a priest. I, too, know how lucky I am to be even indirectly associated with this lively and caring community.

My own ministry has taken me far beyond the boundaries of parish life. Now that my priesthood has been recognized officially by the diocese, many people expect me to be looking for my own position as rector of some parish. "Don't you want a church of your own?" I'm asked again and again. The world is my church, the whole *shebang* of the universe is my parish. And my ministry, centered at Wisdom House, takes me on surprise journeys among fascinating people all over the country. I am a kind of priest-at-large. The travel this involves is sometimes tiring, but the excitement and adventure and real interest of my ministry are benefits that I highly value. I admire Phil for his gifts as a parish priest. He supports me in my ministry as pilgrim priest. We're different people who delight in each other's uniqueness, personally and professionally.

Phil used to say that my ministry was to go ahead of the wagon train to scout out the frontiers of the future, and that his ministry was to stay with the mainstream to encourage the travellers through the transition. I liked the frontier analogy, and would always add my own observation that our arrangement was particularly good, because the scout could always go back to the train and sleep with the wagon master whenever she wanted to!

Three years ago, after spending three years as a deacon, I was ordained to the priesthood—in the same year but not in the same way as Phil. He had employment after his "regular" ordination. And even though I had just completed my doctor of philosophy degree while serving as associate chaplain at Northwestern University, I was to have no employment after my "irregular" ordination. This was especially difficult for me, not only because I was eager to use all the years of academic and professional training, but because it was a time in my life when I needed to be professionally and economically productive for my own sense of self-worth. I knew that the controversy following the Philadelphia ordinations would make it difficult for me to find employment, but I was not aware to what extent this would be true. I didn't expect to be offered a parish position, but I had hoped to be able to secure a seminary or university teaching position and was very disappointed when this didn't happen.

It was Good Friday, 1975, when I went to stand in an unemployment line for the first time. It was a genuinely humiliating experience, no less so for blue collar workers than for professionals loaded with credentials—a public admission of being "all dressed up with no place to go." Interestingly, the State of Minnesota recognized my priesthood that Good Friday before the Episcopal Diocese of Minnesota. The small compensation that was granted didn't come from taxpayers' pockets as some scandalized male clergy suggested at the time (even if it had, *I* was and am also a taxpayer!), but from my previous employment as a scholar by Northwestern University, and as a clergyperson in the Diocese of Minnesota. During the next year-and-a-half, I supported myself in a variety of functions for which I received stipends ranging from nothing to not much. For the rest, I depended on benefits from my past and on the livelihood that Phil shared with me.

It was a full year after my ordination to the priesthood before I could recognize the positive side of my unemployment. I had been working up to a crisis for several months when, one day, I said to Phil, "I can't stand it anymore. I'm tired of being wasted. I'm tired of waiting around for somebody to give me a job. What am I going to do?"

"Get a job," said Phil. "Anything. Only please stop resenting me for earning money and enjoying my work."

He was right. It wasn't fair to him, my going through this emotional backwash, blaming him for having what I wanted

6

instead of enjoying the fact that at least one of us wasn't frustrated. But in my heart I knew that it wouldn't do for me just to "get a job." I wanted more than money. I wanted professional dignity.

I have always known that parish ministry didn't appeal to me. And through my early years in the ministry, I discovered that most conventional forms of ministry didn't appeal to me. I never connected ordination with a particular kind of job. For me, it had to do with a consecrated life, a quality of living as a caring, sacramental person. I was open to creating my own form of ministry. In the beginning, I integrated diaconal or pastoral ministry with my commitment to an ecumenical religious community, and I lived it out within the academic community and the artistic community that both had a claim on my time and energy as a graduate student and a serious young poet.

But after my ordination to the priesthood, I lost this sense of value and enthusiasm in discovering my own style of ministry. I became concerned with my place in the Church and in society as a serious professional woman. All I could think of, with some bitterness, was that I had training, education, and certain gifts and skills, and I was being wasted.

A chronic headache was my body's way of telling me what I was doing to myself. I began to see that I was responsible for my own life, work, and sanity, and that I was becoming more self-destructive than creative in my response to what was a genuinely oppressive situation. Was I just going to sit back and be overcome by the oppression of the Church, and of a professional market in which I found myself to be at the wrong time? I began to see that I had a choice. I could choose not to be a victim, not to be helpless and hopeless. I could choose to fight back by using my situation as an opportunity to re-define and re-create myself—as a woman, as a priest, and as a professional person. When it came to a live or die decision, I could still choose to live. What was facing me was quite literally the challenge to save my own life.

So one winter night in 1975, I stood up in our family room, wiped the tears of self-pity and despair off my cheeks, and declared to the world, "I *won't* be wasted."

I had decided to change my life, and the most basic change of all was in my own attitude. As long as I accepted someone else's definition of me, I had no power in my own life. According to the Church, I was "irregular," and according to some, I wasn't even *valid!* According to the State, I was unemployed. There was certainly more to me than these negative and specious descriptives. I decided to find out just what there really was to me. This meant taking my own power to reject what was evil and destructive in those whose power over me had been to define me negatively, and to begin to use my own power to define myself positively.

With the help of a perceptive spouse and supportive friends, I was able to put myself back on the right track, to create and claim my own values, and to relate to institutions out of my own sense of strength and worth, rather than their sensed desire for me to be weak and unimportant.

The first thing that I did to free myself was to decide that society's system of acknowledging worth with money was not necessarily legitimate. In fact, it was damaging and inaccurate. Human value isn't measured by sliding scale salaries, and income is not a fixed criterion for a person's contribution to society. As long as I lived with someone who was in a position to offer me financial support, I could take my own time in discovering new ways to contribute to society without worrying about getting paid enough for my efforts.

Then I decided that I really did value freedom over money, and that I could use the freedom of my situation to develop my own rhythms of work and play, public participation and private life.

Since that time I have enjoyed a rich diversity of experience in my professional life as a priest, a poet, a feminist, an academician in the performing arts (my degrees are in speech and drama with emphasis on a theology of aesthetics), and as a beginning psychotherapist.

The major part of my out-of-town work is with universities, conducting feminist theology workshops, programs on religion and the arts, giving poetry readings, participating in Oral Interpretation Festivals, and lecturing various classes in areas such as Women in the Church, Women in Literature, the Philosophy or Psychology of Religious Experience. I do similar things on seminary campuses, where I've also conducted journal writing seminars, meditation and contemplative prayer workshops, and retreats.

Local Roman Catholic, Protestant, and Episcopal parishes have invited me as guest preacher over the past few years. I've also been asked to conduct adult education seminars in such varied topics as the Sexuality of Jesus, Russian Spirituality and Iconography, and Liturgical Drama. For two years now I've worked with a speech professor from Macalester College in the Practical School of Speaking sponsored by a local parish to train liturgical readers in the theology and basic skills of their ministry of the Word, and as leaders in worship.

Some of the more rewarding things I've done in recent years have taken me miles from home to find myself among a group of strangers who, through shared values and visions, quickly become friends. A great network of women and men at work to re-humanize and re-Christianize the churches now exists all over the country.

One of the most exciting and productive links in this network is the Institute of Women Today, founded in 1975 by Sister Margaret Ellen Traxler. Margaret has exerted enormous energy in creating an international faculty of professional women to conduct workshops for women around the country in law, education, theology, psychology, and government. The most effective work of the Institute has been among American Third World women and women in prison. The aim of the Institute is to raise the consciousness of women regarding the possibilities for womanpower in the world, and to teach and encourage women to self-actualize this power with one another in their own situations.

It was my great privilege to work with Margaret Ellen and other gifted and sensitive faculty members for three of the Institutes in the Midwest last year. I am sure that the other faculty members will agree wholeheartedly with me that those of us called upon to teach in our own areas of expertise learned more from each other and from other participating women in the Institutes than we were able to offer. We experienced the richness of the women's movement within religious institutions, where Jewish and Christian women are united in their dedication to bring spirituality and humane principles back together again within our own traditions. We also experienced what the religious women's movement has done to make ecumenism a reality. The question, "Am I my sister's sister?" urges us across denominational boundaries for survival and for the sanctification of the redemptive gifts we have to offer our institutions as women of faith.

When I am at home, my ministry is no less stimulating than when I am on the road. Wisdom House is the name of the center in Minneapolis for Ecumenical Oblates, the religious community to which Phil and I belong. It's also where we live. And it's also my church, for the whole second story is a wide open, warmly carpeted, wood-panelled, earth-toned room which is a natural sacred space that serves as a chapel where I celebrate the Eucharist with an ecumenical community every Wednesday evening. We have had Passover Meals, baptisms, special liturgies, and several weddings here. Wisdom House—called such because we need Wisdom most— is also the place where my formal ministry of healing takes place as I give my professional energy to women as a psychotherapist.

Recently I worked with a client who is a clergywoman, an Episcopal deacon seeking priesthood. She had just been turned down by an official diocesan committee having the power to grant or withhold ordination. In her case, the committee made its decision not on the basis of her own merits, but because of the prejudicial effect created by another situation. This, unfortunately, is not a rare experience, but it causes a feeling of complete helplessness and rage in the person who becomes the victim of such unfair and irrational circumstances. I watched this woman heal herself by confronting her pain faithfully through her own rage ritual, and I firmly believe that the truth and power of her work actually reached the spirits of the persons who had caused her pain. I believe this absolutely in light of the Christian doctrine of the communion of saints, and of Jung's understanding of the communication system between souls in what he called the collective unconscious. If a hand in the Body of Christ reaches out in anguish, the eyes must see it. When my client called the following day to tell me that the committee had reversed its judgment, I affirmed her faith and power as an important part of the community of Christ: "It was your magic. They heard you. The complete truth of your whole being when you spoke your pain and despair into the universe with such integrity and authenticity—that had to reach them, move them. You can never force your own resurrection by getting ahead of your process. All you can do is be faithful to your own death, when that is what's facing you. Because you have the courage to meet and go through your death, your resurrection will come, as spring follows winter."

I know this to be true from my own experience in relationship to the Church. By suffering with faith and allowing ourselves to pass all the way through pain and death, we can always discover more life on the other side. The completion of this perennial process requires that we know the moment when to let go of our pain and are willing also to sacrifice our suffering in order to truly claim new life. Letting go has

11

taught me about myself and about ministry.

Through the process of experiencing rejection by the institutional Church, I came to realize what I didn't want in ministry. I didn't want to be a bureaucrat, a business administrator, a power figure, a competitive politician. Now I am coming to realize what I do want. I want to be a healer, a companion in the courageous journeys of individuals toward their own wholeness as persons created uniquely in God's image. For me, the way continues to be through an active merger of the creative process, as in poetry and the dance, the healing process enacted in the drama of psychotherapy, and the sacramental process experienced within a community of faith and worship. My choice and challenge lie in creating a ministry for others out of these elements, which has meaning not only for myself, but for those whose lives I touch and whose lives touch mine. I've come to have a kind of faith in my own ability to survive and grow through the darkest times with the love and support of others who care about me and share my life. Because of them, and because of my own resources, I have a sense of the Holy Spirit among us. My hope is to communicate this in such a way as to help you affirm your belief in your own journey, in the darkness as well as the light.

Parents

I am an American woman, half Russian, part Celtic, one-sixty-fourth Osage Indian. And I am a priest on the growing edge of the Episcopal Church. My name is Alla, a common Russian name I inherited from my mother.

Russians, like people of many other cultures, believed in former days that the mystery and meaning of a person's existence are contained and carried in the name. I'm personally intrigued with the primitive custom of naming a child by the word that is spoken in the birth room as the newborn takes its first breath. Some holy person makes an utterance and that inspired sound becomes the name that holds sacred meaning for the child's whole life.

The mystery and meaning of my name, Alla, are bond up with the word I specially associate with it: *Alleluia—Praise to the One Who Is.*

My second name is Renée, the feminine form of my father's name. It has a double meaning: it comes from the Latin word *renata,* meaning reborn, and from the Gaelic *Irené,* the Goddess of Peace.

My family name is Bozarth, the anglicized form of the French words, *beaux arts*—beautiful art. Campbell, the other part of my hyphenated last name, is my spouse's family name. When we joined our lives in marriage we joined our names to be an accurate symbol of the way we interpret our relationship.

This is the story of my calling, and I have always felt a meaningful link between my calling and my name. To begin with, I perceive my calling as the making of my life into an Alleluia. I think it was St. Augustine who is supposed to have said that the Christian should be an Alleluia from head to foot.

The process of discovering what this means has taken me down many passages, both light and dark, and finally it has led me across the threshold into the priesthood. My understanding of my middle name has helped me through the darker passageways by recalling me to self-renewal, the primary human creative act of giving birth to ourselves again and again out of all our little deaths. From this rebirth comes peace, not the false peace of mere inaction, but the peace of wholeness, of everything working together well.

And finally, my appreciation of my family name, "beautiful art," has probably been responsible at some pre-conscious level for plunging me into poetry, feet first and arms flying, only to find in those unlikely waters the tonic that has healed me a thousand times over and taught my spirit to sing in harmony and dissonance alike—to sing, if necessary, not only with my body's breath, but with its blood.

This is the steadying backdrop of the not-always steady tale I am about to tell.

The personal history in which my vocation to the priesthood was formed is actually older than I am. Each of my parents, in different ways, strongly influenced the formation of my artistic, moral, and spiritual sensibilities. I have to begin with their stories in order to make sense of my own, for on the personal level as well as the collective, I am part of a whole that is made of much more than my own experience.

My mother was born into the Russian aristocracy in Odessa, a town on the Black Sea, in 1909. Her father was a nobleman in the land-owning gentry, and he became an officer in the White Army. I never knew anything more than this about my maternal grandfather until shortly before my mother's death when I was twenty-five. Mother suggested to me, perhaps when she thought I was old enough to take it, that her father's life was far more colorful than the family cared to remember. In one way or another (the stories vary here, some having him heroically assassinated by the Bolsheviks, others indicating a less honorable fate), he died, and left my grandmother with three young children.

The family remained on their estate, which was inhabited by German soldiers assigned to the Ukraine until they were withdrawn in 1923, leaving no protection for the household. My grandmother was a woman of steel. On the day the Germans left, neighboring estates were up in flames by noon. Grandmother organized her children's safety with admirable efficiency. They were off the property and en route to Moscow within a few hours. Mother and her older brother stayed on in Moscow while grandmother escaped illegally through Poland with her younger son.

My mother inherited her own mother's steel, which was put fully to the test for the first time when she was on her own in Moscow. She made herself look older than her fourteen years and enrolled in designer's school. A few years later she had obtained a certificate in design, an asset that allowed her to leave Russia legally under a worker's visa. In 1929 she and her older brother were reunited with the rest of the family in Canada. All of them had endured immeasurable hardships with unyielding courage.

I can remember mother's tales of terror by night during the miles between Odessa and Moscow, when they travelled under hay in horse-drawn wagons, and under baggage on freight trains, where a Red soldier's bayonet once came within an inch of her throat.

I believe that my mother's stamina in those years was fed by her enormous creativity. While she was a hard-working

15

student in design and tailoring, she also became involved in the theater in Moscow, where she acquired considerable experience as a professional actor. She was in a Russian motion picture, *Museppa,* filmed in the twenties. Later in Canada she taught herself English, attended night school at McGill University, and joined the Prime Minister's Theater Company—and all of this while helping to support her family in various menial jobs.

In the mid-thirties, riding on her prominence in Canada, mother went to New York in hopes of starting a Broadway career. She had also begun to write professionally, and while waiting for theatrical success, she wrote for King Features in New York City. During this time she became acquainted with the Russian community in Morningside Heights. Fame eluded her, but she took comfort in another kind of romance. It was in the small colony of exiled Russians in Manhattan that mother met the man who became her first husband: Dmitri de Golikov of the royal house of Rhyzhefsky-Smolensky—a real Russian prince.

The prince had a delicate constitution and was advised to seek a more salubrious climate than New York's for the sake of his health. So the couple moved to California shortly after their marriage. My mother continued to pursue her dramatic career in the bright lights of Hollywood. She made several screen tests but none of them brought her the big break that every potential movie star needs. She began to turn her creative energy elsewhere and took up painting, sculpting, and textiles, all of which she did quite well. During this time she supported Dmitri and herself as a clothes designer at fashionable Brown's in downtown Los Angeles. In 1945 Dmitri died of heart failure. My mother was once again on her own. Her more intimate friends grew impatient with her overly extended period of mourning and encouraged her to develop new relationships among the more lively circles of the California crowd.

Meanwhile, my father had his own radio program in Hollywood. At twenty-two his over-the-air voice made listeners think of a more mature Dylan Thomas, and his romantic format of poetry and music attracted shameless devotion from many members of the audience. My mother was among the devotees.

All persons who bear the surname Bozarth are related to one another through a line of descent from two French brothers. These brothers, according to family legend, were given the epithet, *"les frères des beaux arts,"* due to their notoriety as artists of the romantic mode. Their propinquity for illicit love-making eventually caught up with them, and they were forced to flee France for their lives because of an outraged husband in Normandy. The brothers fled to England, where they married and began to propagate their own families. Later on, both brothers and their families emigrated to Quebec, perhaps finding the French Canadian atmosphere more congenial than the English climate.

The descendants of one brother travelled southward into the United States and settled in Virginia. Members of this branch of the family tended to go into law and medicine. The descendants of the other brother migrated south to New Orleans, and then north to Missouri. This western branch of the family produced at least one member of the clergy in every generation down to and including my own.

My paternal grandfather had been a roaming Reorganized Latter Day Saint preacher. There were Methodists and Mormons and even one Roman Catholic before him. My father and I are the only Bozarth clergy who claim succession in the same denomination. We are an ecumenical brood of independent believers.

My father claims that he always wanted to be a monk, even during his mostly Methodist childhood. (He came from a mixed family: his mother was Methodist for a while.) Instead of this, fortunately for me, his life took another course.

17

When he was nine his mother piled him, his two brothers, and baby sister into an old jalopy and drove westward from Missouri to Washington state, where they settled down in Olympia, the state capital.

It was during the last lap of the Depression that my father began his career in radio broadcasting at the age of fifteen. My grandmother worked in the shipyards and at a T.B. sanitorium to support her family during the end of the Depression and the start of World War II. She also kept a boarding house. Her three sons did what they could to contribute. My father took a job at the local radio station, where his vocal and intellectual gifts were quickly utilized.

By the time he was nineteen, he had published two slim volumes of poetry. That same year his mother sent him to San Antonio, Texas, to recover from the debilitating effects of chronic asthma, a disease nurtured by the damp Pacific Northwest. Through contacts he made in the artistic and literary communities in San Antonio, my father went to Hollywood to establish himself in radio with his own program, "Of Words and Verse."

My mother was enchanted with young René Bozarth's voice and artistic personality. She began attending the drama classes he offered through his radio station. He, in turn, became intrigued with the beautiful Russian princess, whose grief as a young widow added to her exotic mystique. After one kiss on the cheek they cruised out to Santa Catalina Island to be married.

I was conceived on Mariposa ("Butterfly") Street across from the Biltmore Hotel in Los Angeles while my mother was a Hollywood designer and my father was a radio broadcaster. The following year, shortly before my birth, my parents moved to Portland, Oregon, where my father took a new job with radio station KWJJ. I was born on Ascension Day, May 15, 1947, with Pacific Ocean and Cascade Mountains to the west and east of me.

The religious affiliation of my parents at the time of my birth was vague. My father had had a brief romantic encounter with the Old Catholic Church in Hollywood, but the relationship was broken off by disillusionment on his part. My mother had been equally at home in the Russian Orthodox and Lutheran Churches in the Ukraine as a child. The instinct that both my parents had for drama and ritual was probably a strong factor in their decision to have me chrismated (baptized and confirmed) in the Russian Orthodox Church. When I was six months old, I was received into the Christian community in the tiny church of St. Nicholas on Mallory Street at the edge of Portland's black neighborhood.

The service lasted for two hours. My mother made the *Batushka* ("Little Father," as the Russians call their priests) warm the baptismal water to body temperature before she permitted him to christen me with it. The Orthodox baptismal rite includes anointment with oil (chrism) and symbolic acceptance of the gospel. This latter ritual is enacted by the priest's placing the large Book of the Gospels over the infant's face to be kissed. My American grandmother, who was not sure about any of these strange goings-on, chose the moment when I was supposed to kiss the gospels to express her concern. The book was considerably larger than my whole body, and she must have thought that the priest had simply dropped it on top of me for no good reason. "My God," she muttered to my father, "that does it. He's thrown the book at her." Afterwards my Russian grandmother took my American grandmother aside to reassure her that their granddaughter would suffer no permanent damage from the event.

I consider it a capital injustice that the first three years of my life, which I don't remember, were among the most glamorous. I knew or was known by some exceptional per-

19

sons when I was a wee small thing. When I was two, a Portland newspaper recorded a conversation I had with the great socialist, Norman Thomas, who was visiting at my house one day. Other remarkable people with whose lives mine collided momentarily were Eleanor Roosevelt, Arthur Rubenstein, the conductor/violinist Boris Sirpo, and Senator Richard Neuberger of Oregon. I can scarcely recall one or two encounters with Boris Sirpo, but I remember nothing at all of any of the others. Naturally all these people weren't interested in me just for my own sake; I came along with their business affiliation with my parents, especially with my father through his radio work, for it was his professional pleasure to interview and entertain prominent persons.

It's another injustice of fate that as an infant I was more fluent in foreign languages than I am now. Mother taught me to speak in Russian, German, French, and a little Spanish, so that I had quite a reputation for it. My first grade teacher put an end to it when she explained to my mother how confusing it would be for the poor child to learn to read and write in book English with all those other languages floating around in her head. But my chances for a glamorous life-style ended earlier than this, and that came about indirectly as the result of my father's contact with Senator Neuberger.

Senator Richard Neuberger of Oregon introduced my father to a man named Corwin Calavan. He was an Episcopal priest. It was through my father's emerging friendship with him that we were introduced to the Episcopal Church.

No one in my family has ever been known for lukewarmness. We are passionate livers to a person, and tend to go all the way when something seems worthy of commitment. When I was three years old my father left a career in radio to become an Episcopal priest. After a farewell celebration arranged by his colleagues, he joined the Episcopal Church and was off to seminary in the same month to study for ordination.

20

We lived in the home of my Russian grandmother in Vancouver, British Columbia, while my father studied at the Anglican Theological College nearby. My mother began to pursue seriously her career as an artist. My time was divided between being her assistant and chief critic, and mascot of the seminary.

In 1951 my father was ordained to the diaconate and we returned to Oregon, where he became vicar of a small mission in the town of Gresham, eleven miles east of Portland near Mt. Hood. The mission consisted of about ten families, including ours. No church building existed, but one of the members of the little congregation offered his place of business for public services. It was a funeral parlor. I embarrassed my father terribly one Sunday morning when I asked, "Why is that man sleeping in that suitcase?" After that, Mr. Bateman carefully locked all the doors leading to the business section of the establishment well before Sunday services were to begin.

Later that same year father was ordained to the priesthood and the congregation of St. Luke the Physician had broken ground for its church building. My father became rector of that parish, which he served for a total of thirteen years.

Ever since I was a small child, ministry has been a natural part of my life. Since I had no sisters or brothers, I was a privileged stowaway in the adult world from the beginning. It was an astonishing world of which each of my parents showed me a different side.

My mother's busy life was an arena for my imagination and cultural development. For a time, when I was still very young, she worked with the Lutheran Welfare Agency in Portland. It was her responsibility to find homes and sponsors for thousands of Eastern European, Cuban, and Indonesian families seeking resettlement in America. I met many of these folk, since mother would always assume personal responsibility for their emotional comfort upon arrival into a strange community. Because mother had the advantage of being able to speak several languages, she functioned as intercultural interpreter and liaison between the families and their American sponsors until the two had developed for themselves a satisfactory means of friendly communication. This was my mother's ministry. Even I, as young as I was, could observe its great value to those she served.

Despite the time and energy that her Christian social service work required, my mother managed to maintain her creative pursuits in the arts. Among her more serious endeavors, she indulged herself in an occasional frivolity. When I was six years old we both took violin lessons together for a very short time. Both of us must have decided rather early on that whatever artistic medium we were suited for, it was not the violin.

My father's ministry also often included me. When I was four or five he began to take me along on parish calls. I was fascinated by the grown-ups whose homes we visited. I was dimly aware that these interesting individuals went to our church and that my father had a responsibility toward them.

Both of my parents were Christian activists. They were living and usually unself-conscious examples to me and to others. As soon as I became old enough to understand that my parents' lives were lives of service, I decided that my life would be that, too. It had obvious rewards as well as difficulties. My growing-up years were challenging because of the lives my parents shared with me. Something was always going on somewhere, and I was learning effortlessly and unconsciously from the examples of my parents. Each of them had the capacity to keep things stirred up in their areas of commitment.

There was, for example, a nursing home next to our parish church, separated from it only by a narrow driveway. The two institutions had been mutually indifferent toward one another for years when, one day, my father brought a newspaper article to the attention of some of the parishioners. It was reported that the owners of the nursing home next door had been arrested for drug and alcohol abuse, cruelty, and professional neglect of the patients. Some members of the parish were horrified by the situation and felt that the parish family had a moral responsibility toward its elderly neighbors. The vestry (parish council) determined that the parish corporation could not assume ownership and administration of the facility, so my father sought the advice of his bishop. He was told that if he had such a ministry in mind, the thing to do would be to found an order of monks or nuns to take on the work. In 1958 the Society of St. Paul became the first order of Episcopal Brothers in the diocese of Oregon. The Brothers purchased the nursing home from its new owners and began a caring ministry of nursing and administration at St. Jude's Home for the aged ill.

The rectory where I grew up was surrounded by St. Jude's Home and St. Luke's Parish Church to the north, and by the original monastery to the south. Just east of this complex was Holy Trinity School, another facility that the Brothers operated for several years, and where I attended seventh and eighth grades. We lived in the rectory for eight years, until my father resigned as parish rector in 1964 to devote himself full time to the work of the Society of St. Paul. His was an unusual position since he had founded a monastic order without himself joining it (for he was a married man with family, besides being the active rector of a small town parish). Only indirectly his youthful dreams of becoming a monk had been fulfilled, yet in this way he was able to keep one foot in each world to the enrichment of the other. The strain of his several ministries wore on his health over the years, for his energy output was total in all directions. For him the challenge was in many ways its own reward.

As the parish priest's only child and as the daughter of a

23

remarkable woman, I grew up in the shadow of each of my parents, and I was often considered the extension of one or the other of them. Each in her or his own way cast a special cultivating light on my greening vines. Against the light and shade of their influence I was called upon to define myself, related to, participating in, yet separate from their lives.

My parents' lives were in fact separated from each other. Strong individual temperaments caused them to work better apart than together. They began to see less of one another when I was fifteen and my father made his headquarters in a modest house next door to the new monastery.

When the Brothers moved their monastery to the small town of Sandy, eleven miles east of Gresham under the shadow of the great white mountain, a single-story blue house adjacent to the property became a second home for my father and me. It was called Charter House. My mother maintained her residence and work in Gresham, and the three of us would get together two or three times a week, either in Gresham or in Sandy. Charter House became a guest house for the monastery and it gradually became my home. I was in the position of providing hospitality for visitors—a task I very much enjoyed. I also used Charter House for my own purposes. Friends of mine often found refuge there during times of personal crisis. It gained a reputation as a place of safety and renewal for many people, especially for women undergoing critical transition. In 1966, eleven persons in the process of divorce came to Charter House at different times for retreat and regathering of inner resources, as did several women and men in process of leaving religious orders. Word of its availability had spread. I felt somewhat dismayed by the need for such a place, but at the same time I was grateful for my father's support of my own developing ministry.

Meanwhile I prayed the daily offices with the Brothers

24

and assimilated more and more of my religious environment. I had absorbed an abundance of literature on Western spirituality and religious life, and had come to perceive in myself a vocation to some form of religious life that had been taking shape all during my childhood. I also began consciously to integrate Western spirituality with Russian spirituality, turning back to my roots in that tradition.

When my father became an Episcopalian, my mother and I considered ourselves Episcopalians too. I was officially received into the Episcopal church when I was ten years old. Mother saw to it that my ties with the Russian Church were never broken. Together we attended the Divine Liturgy in the Russian Church every Christmas and Easter, and would often go to Vespers on other occasions, and then visit with *Matushka* and *Batushka* Sherotsky afterwards. (My last visit to *Matushka* was after the death of her spouse and just before my own ordination and wedding. She wanted to give me an ordination/wedding present. I cherish the two small, old, bent silver spoons that came out of Imperial Russia and fed many mouths in transit before they were given to the Sherotskys, who had no spoons, by another refugee couple one night in an Austrian train station long ago.)

Especially during all the Easters of my childhood, I was reminded of my Russian heritage and the deep roots I have in a culture I've never really known. It was during Easter time that mother would prepare all the traditional paschal food— the wonderful tall standing sweet bread, *koolitch,* baked in vertical molds till the round brown tops rose high in honor of the rising Christ, and *paschka,* the creamy cheese-and-raisin mixture served in a glorious festive mound. The Easter salutation in Russian would ring in the air, thrilling the hearer with its joyous, triumphal sound:

"Christos vos kresye!" Christ is risen!
"Voiestyenoe vos kresye!" The Lord is risen indeed!

25

I had known Russian spirituality by intuition and experience as a child—a vividly colorful, sensual, warm, and vibrant spirit that poured spontaneously out of the hearts of the Russian people. With the establishment of an Anglican religious order next door to us, I also had the opportunity to discover the treasures of Western spirituality. Later, I was to understand my vocation to ecumenism as the organic interplay of a personal enrichment from Eastern and Western sources, an interplay rising spontaneously out of my own early lived experience of both traditions.

Friends

My early childhood was no more pious than was good for me. I felt naturally close to God as children do, but I had no use for church. My mother complained in her diary that I made Sundays miserable for her because I hated to go to church, just like most healthy little kids. It was boring. Few grown-ups are honest enough to admit that they resent being bored in church, but children very rightly won't put up with it.

One Sunday morning when I was nine years old I was standing near the doorway in the back of the church, probably day-dreaming. Suddenly I became aware of a beautiful woman's face in front of me. The face was speaking to me.

"Are you all alone here? You can sit with us, if you'd like."

I saw before me a striking woman of about twenty-three, entirely grown-up, her long curly black hair framing her clear face like a black lion's mane. Her huge, penetrating brown eyes called me out of my dreams more powerfully than her gentle voice. I didn't know it then, but the most important woman in my life had just introduced herself.

Years later, Pauline told me how embarrassed she was that day when one of the parishioners told her the little girl she felt sorry for was the rector's daughter. I don't remember whether or not I sat with her family that morning. Probably not, as I liked to be able to move around during the services and generally found a free space near the front or back of the church near a door. In fact, I don't remember very much about Pauline until several years later, though I clearly recall her two tiny daughters whom I sometimes watched over in the nursery.

When I was thirteen, I had an extraordinary religious experience. In the old days, it might have been called a vision. I call it an opening, a breaking forth into and out of my psyche of the overpowering love of God. The whole depth dimension of eternity dropped down and absorbed me in the qualitative experience of the holy. It began with a particular experience while I was praying. It was as if a whole inner world suddenly revealed itself and drew me inside, a world so large that for some months afterward, the sky looked small to me.

This inner world was peopled with beings whom I recognized as friends and helpers, beings who offered me joy beyond expression, but who were not above commonplace humor. One of them, for instance, would see to it that I didn't sleep in on mornings when I wanted to attend the Eucharist. Since I have always been genetically disinclined toward mornings, this was no small task. On these occasions, I would hear someone saying to me, "Get up! Get up!" and knew immediately that it was this particular friend I had in the communion of saints who had undertaken this duty for me, the duty of a caring but necessarily impatient parent. "All right, all right," I'd groan, and roll myself out of bed, a very bleary-eyed and ungrateful recipient of this kindness.

Although I had an initial experience of the holy—a kind of conversion experience in that it turned my life onto a different course toward inner realities—my experience of the numinous was not a one-time thing. In fact, it went on for years. Suddenly my family couldn't get me *out* of church. This

28

intense relationship and increasing intimacy that I experienced with God in prayer enriched my imagination and whole psychic sensibility to the point where the inner world seemed more real to me than the outer one. It was certainly more interesting. I think that during that time, I was not really at home on the earth, or in my own body. My sense of displacement made me aware of the limitations of the physical side of life, rather than the incarnational power and holiness of it that I was to experience much later.

The next time that I actually remember meeting Pauline was soon after I began to live this new existence. She was pregnant with her fourth child. What a sight she was, huge with life, dressed in a bright red winter coat that fell full around her form, revealing such incongruously thin hands and legs, her narrow oval face draped with a red winter shawl! I thought she was Christmas incarnate. It was twilight on the cold winter evening of December 29, 1960, after a Service of Carols in St. Luke's Church. We met each other outside, and there was between us such a stirring of recognition as I have experienced only once since then in my thirty years. We saw in each other's souls with x-ray vision, way down deep into the awesome places of each other's hearts. There was a moment of surprise between us, and then we both began to speak at once. When could we get together. How soon? For how long—a whole day? Yes, yes, at least a day. Three days later we shared a meal, and then opened up our hearts to each other in a sharing of our lives that has only deepened through the years, and that will carry us, we're sure, to the day of our deaths and into eternity.

We saw each other often over the next few years, as often as possible. I'm sure that our relationship confused our families. A grown-up married woman with a family, and a young girl who lived like a nun—what could they possibly have in common to talk about? We both kept spiritual journals, turning to writing to assuage the loneliness we both had

29

felt in our spiritual journeys. We had discovered companions in each other, and what we had to talk about were all the secret loves and longings of our souls for God, for a love that was enduring, absolute, divine.

The miracle of our relationship is that through the years each of us has undergone astonishing changes from those early days, and yet we have never grown apart from each other, only closer together, even when our ideological views seemed on the surface to be vastly different.

Pauline's last child, Veronica, was born in 1962, and named after me—named Veronica because that name means "true image," and I had chosen the name for its meaning to be my religious name. I became Veronica's godmother. She is a beautiful young woman herself, now. I see her every summer and delight in her growth and development as much as I have delighted in her mother's during the long interweaving of our lives.

Pauline is a poet and a writer of fiction. She encouraged me to write poetry myself, from the very start of our relationship. I began to write when I was thirteen, first the journals and then the poetry. I imitated the style of my favorite writer, St. John of the Cross, his beautiful love poems to God translated by Roy Campbell. My imitations were immature and pretty poor. When Pauline and I get together even now and have had a few brandies, we'll start reciting lines from my old poems in high chanting descant, splitting our sides over their super-serious style. Not that we mock the sentiments behind them, only the language. Pauline was using free forms in her poetry while I was still struggling with sonnets and sestinas. Arrogant and rigid as youth often is, I would listen to one of her new poems and my only comment would be, "It has interesting syntax, doesn't it?"

Pauline was a mother to my soul in the beginning of our relationship. Later on, when her life came apart through divorce and the poverty of a single parent putting herself through college and raising five children with no support, I became her mother. The difference in our ages has never made the slightest difference in our ability to respond to each other's needs. We have been sisters, mothers, daughters, and dearest friends to each other. As my religious quest took me more deeply into the institutional Church, Pauline's took her out and away from it, back into her Jewish roots, and then through Eastern mystical religions to the recognition of the Motherhood of God. Having come through this spiritual cycle, she shared her new spiritual perceptions with me only to discover that I, too, have come to honor the feminine in the divine, through an entirely different cycle of my own. We celebrate the miracle of our growth, which has taken us down different roads but always kept us in sight of each other, able to give greetings of loving affirmation to one another from our separate paths—and finally, to discover that our paths have brought us to the same place in the end, which is only another beginning for us.

While God had given my soul a mother and sister in Pauline from whom I received healing grace and growing wisdom, I had another need that she couldn't fulfill. My soul needed a brother as well.

The summer after I turned fourteen, a young school teacher from Pennsylvania came to join the monastery. He was called Brother Barnabas. All that Pauline had been to me as a sister, he became as a brother.

It's difficult for me to describe my loneliness during those years, mostly because it was such an internal, intangible thing. I hadn't noticed being lonely before, even though I had always spent much of my time by myself from early childhood on. This is the usual "only-child syndrome." I was comfortable in the adult world, and among my peers in school I was withdrawn, being more a miniature adult than an easy playmate. I had worked this out pretty well for myself. School had always bored me; I found it interesting only because of the one or two close friends whom I consistently found each year. When I was three I had one good friend in the neighborhood. In school I sought out one special person I could be close to, and always concentrated on developing a particular good relationship rather than trying to mingle in with everyone. I guess this is a pattern I've followed all my life. My sense of personal privacy was well formed very early. But I was never lonely.

It was when this pattern of privacy, balanced by very close relationships with a few, became coupled with the introspection of my teens that I no longer found satisfaction in friendships with my peers. My chosen aloneness became lonely as well for the first time. Because of the powerful internal movement that was going on inside me I had an emotional need to express and communicate the rich contemplative experiences that were changing my life. I felt that there was no one among my peers who would understand any of it. So I considered myself well blessed when I found a few caring and responsive adults who were sensitive to my spiritual and emotional needs. I began to develop strong bonds with them, happy to discover that they had similar needs for sharing at a deep level where I could meet them.

My spiritual awakening occurred after the Society of St. Paul had been in existence for several years. I began to pray the daily Offices with the Brothers and to attend Mass regularly. Brother Andrew, who was one of the founding Brothers, was like a blood brother to me. I first knew him when I was nine and he was nineteen. In a sense, we grew up together. He was a good, comfortable friend. The other Brothers were kind and accepting toward me. But my relationships with them were that of little sister to big brothers. My soul still craved someone special.

Then Barnabas came into my life. Again there was an inexplicable intuitive bond between us that we both recognized. Perhaps we both feared it as well. We were young enough to be vulnerable but old enough to be aware of it. So we formed an unspoken agreement to be sister and brother to one another's soul, expressing our love and understanding of each other through a spiritual bond of prayer and counsel. I learned that "Barnabas" meant "Consolation," and I declared him my personal Consolation, someone to reach out to, someone to touch my loneliness, someone I could also touch in some healing way. Our communion has also deepened through the years. We have both grown into more complete human beings because we've always been there for each other.

By the time I was fourteen I had decided that I wanted to give my life completely to God, and the only way I knew of to do this was by becoming a nun. Given my intense nature, once I'd made the decision, I wanted to act on it immediately. My poor parents—they had a fourteen-year-old daughter who wanted to be a nun, and not only a nun, but a cloistered, contemplative nun, and not only did she want all this, but she wanted it *now,* without further delay. My mother thought I was going through some phase of religious mania, and my father just thought I was enduring an outrageously romantic attack of adolescence. Neither of them took me seriously until they began to see that I was serious and not about to give up. I began writing the Superior of the Franciscan Poor Clares, asking her to admit me as a postulant. She wrote back very gentle but firm letters telling me it would be wise to wait awhile. I was frustrated beyond words. My parents didn't understand me, my teachers didn't understand me, and I was a mystery to my peers. But I had Pauline, and I had Barnabas. No matter how mad my desires must have seemed to everyone else, and how pained my parents were to see me so determined and so frustrated, there were at least two people in the world who never rejected any part of me, who accepted unquestioningly. This didn't mean that Barnabas in his way and Pauline in hers didn't try to reason with me too, but when I told them that I had a religious vocation, they believed me. They never tried to talk me out of that.

I began to seek out affirmation from other religious women. I had a voluminous correspondence with a Carmelite nun who was a sister of a friend of my priest confessor. But I wanted face-to-face contact with women whom I felt had callings similar to what I perceived mine to be. There was a Roman Catholic community of contemplative nuns in Portland, the Sisters of the Precious Blood, and I began to attend their public services. Soon I ventured into the parlor to introduce myself to the Sisters. I was intrigued by the cloister and the strange set-up in the parlor where guests sat on one side of the room and the Sisters, in their dramatic red and white habits, sat on the other, a whitewashed lattice work grille in between. If we wanted to pass something back and forth, it had to be small enough to fold or roll up to fit the two-inch squares of the lattice. I met many of the Sisters. They seemed happy enough to have visitors, and they were probably intrigued by such a young woman's dedication to a future in religious life as an Episcopal nun.

When I was sixteen or seventeen I drove to the Monastery of the Precious Blood at least once a week. My mother began to accompany me. She enjoyed the Sisters' services and had a good time visiting with the nuns in the parlor afterward. I made special friends of two of the Sisters—Sister Mary Catherine and Sister Mary of the Holy Spirit, both women in their thirties.

After six or eight months, I began to be aware of stirrings inside the Sisters' monastery. My friend Cathy (Mary Catherine) one day told me about a fascinating young priest who had come to visit them, along with a man who was an important figure in the Charismatic Movement. I found it interesting that Cathy was more interested in the priest than the more colorful charismatic gentleman. A few more months passed and Cathy began to share her restlessness with me, her sense of needing to serve God in a less limiting, more open way of life. This was true. It was also true that Cathy was in love, so I helped my friend make the necessary arrangements in preparing to leave the monastery. Meanwhile, Sister Mary of the Holy Spirit was making her own plans to leave in order to found a more austere but non-enclosed community of contemplative Sisters. The story ended when I saw Mary in Rome at the Center for the Better World Movement the following summer, and several years later at her new convent in South Bend, Indiana, with the dozen or so Sisters who had joined her in this new foundation. A year before that I attended Cathy's wedding to the young priest who had been so fascinating.

Well before the wedding, I had met the young priest myself. He was a very appealing person, fresh and enthusiastic and totally dedicated to God. He, too, was restless and felt confined in his parish ministry as a Roman Catholic priest. It was through him, during this rather turbulent period in his life, that I came to meet, know, and love another woman whom I claim as an eternal friend and soul sister, Mary Corah.

Jerry served as associate pastor of a Roman Catholic parish in northwest Portland. Cathy had told him about our friendship, and Jerry in turn had mentioned me to some of the women in his parish who met regularly for a prayer and study hour. The women expressed a desire to meet me and invited me to pray with them. When I attended their March meeting in 1964, I was taken by two of the women of Assumption parish to the home of Mary Corah who had offered hospitality to the group in her home that month. Mary was sitting on the couch in her living room nursing her infant daughter, Valerie, when we walked in the door.

It was an interesting meeting. One of the women, a neighbor of Mary's, was a newly converted charismatic who had a persistent style about her that dominated the group in a

35

rather unpleasant way. I could tell that Mary especially felt uncomfortable. Everyone was polite, and since no one was willing to argue with Sabrina, she soon calmed down and let other people speak. Mary began to pick my brain near the end of the hour, and I had my first experience of what I have come to love in her—a deliciously candid curiosity about people, and a bold and childlike way of expressing it. Questions, questions, questions! She got her intent freckled face in an even line with my face, fixed her curious blue eyes on me, and without losing contact with baby Valerie on her lap, she set out to discover who I was. There wasn't much time, though, and other people were there too, so we were cut short. But a few days later, Mary called me on the telephone, first to apologize for her overbearing friend who had tried to evangelize the group to her own religious leanings, and then to invite me over for lunch.

My first lunch at Mary's kitchen table was an experience we repeated many times together over the years—the telephone ringing every five minutes, one or the other of her four kids coming in for a snack or mother's attention, a pile of laundry on a chair between us, Mary folding clothes while telling me all about the newest book she'd read. No matter how often I saw Mary, she always had a new book, and there was always a new person in her life whom I just had to meet. Off we'd go in her car, sometimes before I could even get through the door into her house, and I'd be taken to school for a ball game to cheer for her son Paul, or to meet Mr. Ethen, a special friend from church, or "the Green Pope," a delightful octogenarian who supervised all Irish Catholics in the world from his North Vatican Headquarters in a nearby nursing home, with the faithful assistance of his paraplegic friend, Pat.

Mary had so much energy and was so intent on learning everything there was to learn about life and people. She never stopped questioning, examining, making up her mind

36

about this and that. No, the Pope (the Italian one) had no business telling married people how to conduct their sex lives. Yes, birth control was okay even if he said otherwise. And what did I think about charismatics, spiritualism, E.S.P., Salvador Dali, modern dance and home cooking? I knew that someday soon all this imaginative energy would burst forth into a suitable creative medium. So when Mary told me that she had taken up painting and surprised herself by being good at it, I wasn't surprised.

Mary has developed into a talented artist. Her paintings have been on exhibit and attracted enough attention to begin selling. I have four of them now, one of them painted to go with my poem "The Woman at the Well." Even though Mary is a feeling, giving, and often impulsive person, she is probably the most solid, the most anchored of my friends. She has always had a steadying influence on me. While Pauline and I flew together through the heavens, Mary took me to the beach and walked with me in warm wet sand. She has also been both mother and daughter to me through the years. Our love for each other is warm and deep and long, sometimes flaring out like a volcano, sometimes crackling away like a slow, small driftwood fire by the ocean at night. With her, as with all of my closest, oldest friends, I enjoy not only the deepest kind of sharing, but ordinary, silly, fun things as well. Mary's spontaneous generosity and responsiveness to people always teaches me how good life can be at its simplest.

I wish that it were possible for me to honor all of the special people in my life here, but truly each one of them deserves an entire book, not just brief mention such as I can give them in these pages. Pauline and Barnabas and Mary are key people in my formation as a woman, a priest, a poet, a human being. I am grateful for the opportunity to pay public homage to their humanity. For the others—Mary Kay Rowland in the Madonna House Apostolate who deepened and stretched the possibilities of contemplative prayer, the prayer of the heart, the prayer in the desert, for me; Dennise Brown who shared early morning geology classes and late afternoon poetry readings with me at Northwestern University, and who later taught me what it means to live courageously by facing profound transformations in her own life with courage and grace; Kris Minister, an intellectual colleague and companion in the performing arts—for these and for the many others who have touched my life and taught me what it means to be human, I thank God. May we all be blessed with such friends.

Teachers

I was the only kid in Father Parker's eighth grade class at Holy Trinity School who spent lunch hours in church. Thirteen years old and newly in love with God—but I didn't always express my love with grace. The eighth grade class was a pretty rowdy bunch. Father Parker had a special spot in his heart for me, maybe because he had no daughter of his own and I was his brother priest's child. He'd show his affection for me in ways that were sometimes all right and sometimes not. I was pleased when he asked me to fill in for him sometimes reading Victor Hugo's *Les Miserables* to the class after lunch. But one day, when he'd reached his wit's end with some of the more boisterous kids, he threw up his hands, letting the book he was about to read from fall to the floor. No one would settle down for reading time. "I've had it with you," he said to everyone in general. "You clods spend all your time raising hell in here. It's just a good thing for you that Alla goes off to pray for your souls every noontime."

"Hey, just a minute, Sir," I protested. "Don't make me the classroom saint. I go off to pray with the Brothers because I like to. The other kids do what they like." I never really got over being set apart in that way. Nobody wants to be resented for being too good. I notice a trait in myself even now that probably goes back to that incident. My physical

39

appearance often gives people a first impression that I am a porcelain delicacy. If I'm aware that a person has this particular impression of me, I take gleeful delight in saying or doing something totally unexpected and outrageous to throw off the mystique. I do like to keep people on their toes, and I don't like being labelled or boxed in by preconceptions or fixed impressions. Basically, whether from myself or others, I enjoy surprises. And life does provide them.

As an educator, Father Walter Parker was charismatic. His tall, sturdy frame, his reddish hair, eyes that could blaze out like arrows to break your heart with remorse or light up with a laughter so contagious that you couldn't escape it if you were paid to—his whole personal bearing made people want to pay attention, to hear every word. This made his teaching believable, authentic.

But I learned the most from him outside the classroom in those rare moments when I caught him unexpectedly at prayer, his whole body a powerful and moving expression of human longing for God, or watching his way of responding to students, to their deepest human needs for encouragement, affirmation, and care.

When I graduated, a decision had to be made about high school. I had been spoiled by the caring manner of Father Parker and felt certain that I wouldn't find such qualities in public school teachers. I wasn't very thrilled with the alternative, though. There was an Episcopal day and boarding school for girls in downtown Portland that had been founded by the Sisters of St. John the Baptist in my grandmother's day. St. Helen's Hall was the logical place for me to attend high school. But the Sisters had been gone for years, leaving the teaching and administration of the school in the hands of a small faculty of mostly upper class women. The school had a reputation for social snobbery that didn't appeal to me. Furthermore, its student body had a reputation for rowdiness that made the most unmanageable boys in my eighth grade class seem placid and tame.

40

All of my life I have had to eat humble pie when a quick negative judgment had proved plainly wrong. My own lesson on not prejudging or labeling people comes back to me those many times when I do it myself. So it was that when I became a full-time day student at St. Helen's Hall, I discovered that *I* was the snobbish one. I had been guilty of reverse classism—prejudging people only on the basis of their having wealth. The teachers impressed me as being genuinely dedicated, and I found excellent, outgoing friends among my classmates.

Isabel McKirdie was my freshman and sophomore history teacher. What a mind that woman had! The first scholarly mind I had ever experienced, incisive and precise, absorbed in her subject, able to communicate it vividly and imaginatively. Because of her, I have an appreciation of the human drama we call history. But I also have an appreciation for the sheer discipline of refined scholarship, an appreciation that she planted in my brain in often uncomfortable ways. Miss McKirdie was without mercy in her demand for self-dedication and accuracy in the work of her students. She had little tolerance for poetic fantasies. She was, in short, a woman who couldn't be fooled. She was not above humiliating a student who failed to give her total attention to the subject at hand, and her cutting remarks on a paper or test when she felt that a student didn't know her material fully were not always easy to take. The girls in her class had to learn quickly to overcome any tendencies toward easily hurt feelings. Miss McKirdie was the first person in my academic career who ever challenged me. She sized up an individual during the first week of classes, and if she felt that a person's intellectual capabilities were great, she had no tolerance whatever for mediocrity or anything less than sheer excellence.

While Isabel McKirdie was a scholar of the first order, her dedicated friend and colleague, Ruth Rose Richardson, was one of the few genuine intellectuals I have ever known.

41

Miss Richardson taught English Literature, but her field of knowledge covered the spectrum of science and philosophy. Her approach to literature was direct and distinctive. Her demands for scholarly accuracy were no less than Miss McKirdie's, but sensitive to her particular subject of literature, she taught with an amazing balance of sensual appreciation and spiritual intensity.

When I decided at the beginning of my junior year to transfer to a Roman Catholic Dominican school much nearer to my home, Miss Richardson and Miss McKirdie both made me feel valued and wanted as a student and a person. They both told me they hated to see me go, and I was truly moved by the sincerity of the regret they expressed. Being valued by those two women meant more to me than I can say. In fact, I owe it to them that I later chose to commit myself to a creative form of scholarship in my own field of Interpretation, a branch of Speech and Drama, that includes both the performing art and the literary analysis sides of the study and enactment of literature. My doctoral degree is as much theirs as it is mine, for their mutual passion for, and dedication to, learning gave me the incentive and faith to do my own intellectual work. I first learned from them that intellectual passion and imaginative creativity need not exclude each other.

It was because of my own commitment to the poetic process that I got into my academic field. I wanted to improve my work as a poet by matching it with the skilled ear and trained body of a good oral interpreter. (The phrase "oral interpretation" is unfortunate because good interpretation of literature is always much more than "oral." It is an art form that involves the total engagement of the whole person — physical, sensual, spiritual, intellectual, imaginative processes — all working together to make the word into flesh and give it life. For me, this is also a holy process, a theological act — that of *incarnation*.)

One other teacher in my life must be spoken of here. I don't mean to suggest that she is less important in my formation than the three persons I've already described. However, she is so very important she deserves a separate chapter, or more rightly she deserves a place at the heart of my discussion of friends, and later on when I tell you about the development of my religious vocation. Sister Rosaire was instrumental in my life on many levels all at once, even though our time together was relatively short.

At the beginning of my junior year, I was the only non-Roman Catholic student at Marycrest High School. The Sisters welcomed me, expressing a desire for more ecumenical outreach in the school, since Vatican Council II was beginning to have impact on Christians at a grassroots level. I was made to feel at home by students and Sisters alike, especially by Sister Rosaire.

Sister Rosaire was also an English teacher. I studied American and then English literature through her. Her approach to literature was intense yet gentle, like her whole personality. Rosaire had enormous brown eyes that always seemed to be reaching beyond her face to meet the world and its people; they weren't content merely to see, they wanted to touch as well. She was an intensely contemplative person, a spiritual comrade of Thomas Merton, and of her own Dominican Brother Antoninus, a poet and Christian shaman.

Rosaire teased me forever about the time she asked the class to name some of the great works of literature that we'd read, and I popped up with "The *Summa Theologica* of St. Thomas Aquinas!" I had read it because it was among the works in my family's Great Books series, but it really was a bit exhibitionistic to admit to it in front of everyone. Apparently I had touched Rosaire's heart by my innocent precociousness, so she took me under her wing. I shared my poetry with her, and she encouraged me to go on writing. She be-

43

came my special spiritual confidante. She shared with me her love of the vision and writings of Gerard Manley Hopkins. Often she quoted his poem "The Windhover" to me, and in Hopkins' style she spoke of Christ "eastering" in us all.

Sister Rosaire taught me by her example that education is not only outreach, but embodiment. Observing and listening to her, I learned that study can also be a work of art and a form of prayer, and that neither study nor prayer can exist separately from experience, the day-to-day reality of a person's life.

The summer after my graduation from Marycrest, our friendship came into full bloom. We were no longer defined by the roles of teacher and student, and our relationship became free to define itself on its own terms. Rosaire asked me to drive her and another Sister—a science teacher recently, like me, exposed to, and excited by, Teilhard de Chardin—to the Dominican Retreat at McKenzie Bridge in central Oregon for a weekend of rest and prayer.

McKenzie Bridge was a turning point for me in my growth as a poet, a fact that I owe entirely to Sister Rosaire. She had been encouraging me, like my friend Pauline, to try different styles of poetry, to break into free form and allow myself to grow. I had expressed distaste of "modern poetry," covering my own insecurity at the thought of launching out on the unknown waters of my own creativity. How could I abandon the safe, sure womb of standard rhythm, rhyme, and meter?

I was sitting by myself on a rock in the middle of the McKenzie River, which was very narrow and shallow at that point, dazzling with morning sunlight, the dark wet stones around me like swimming animals coming up for warmth on an early June day. I began to write—without rhyme, without strict form—just to write from my heart. Some of the poems I wrote that morning were as stiff and awkward as a newborn colt. Others took to their feet with a degree of grace, and

44

were able to stretch and move on their own. Very shyly, I took the poems to Sister Rosaire, and she read some of them aloud to her friend and the two Dominican Brothers who shared lunch with us. One of the Brothers was a close friend of Antoninus, and he had some understanding of the kind of poetry I had begun to experience in myself. He and Rosaire both told me that I'd made a good beginning, and made me promise not to stop, a confirmation later echoed by Pauline, who read the new poetry with smiles and relief.

One of the poems I wrote at McKenzie Bridge that weekend was among the first of my published poems.

Rapport

The human encounter
is a kiln of exchange;
friendship is
communion and love
in which Charity
is the White Heat
of sharing.

Sisters

Besides the individuals I've described, there were other teachers responsible for my early formation, teachers from whom I learned not only of the human world, but of the transcendent world of the spirit. These teachers reached me through their writings. Among the most important of them, in terms of their powerful effect on my psyche, were the 16th-century Carmelite reformers and mystics, Teresa of Avila and John of the Cross, followed by Thérèse of Lisieux, in the late 19th century. They led me to seek out a religious community in which I could learn still more about the life of the spirit. Through them I met some religious women who not only were Sisters—in that they belonged to traditional religious orders—but who became sisters to me in a spiritual sense, and in the sense of the solidarity of sisterhood spoken of today in the women's movement in Church and society.

The Carmelite writers were persons whose powerful religious experiences I felt were analogous to my own in intensity, if not in kind. Thus I came to believe that I should be a Carmelite. When I mentioned earlier that I wanted to be an enclosed contemplative nun, it was in fact a Carmelite that I wanted to be.

This presented an immediate problem, since there were no Anglican Carmelites anywhere in the world. (There were communities adopting a similar lifestyle, but these were in England.) There was only one contemplative religious order for women in the Episcopal Church in the United States, the Franciscan Order of Poor Clares on Long Island. My greatest problem, I thought at the time, was that I did not want to become a Roman Catholic just to be a Carmelite. The fact that I was only fourteen years old seemed much less of an obstacle, for I had already decided that if Thérèse of Lisieux could be a Carmelite at fourteen, so could I. But it appeared that I would have to be a Poor Clare instead, since that was the closest thing to a Carmelite that my church allowed for.

The Superior of the Poor Clares was a wise and sensible woman. After I'd been pestering her for three years, she finally invited me to spend a few weeks observing the Franciscan life-style first hand. I spent a month at the Poor Clare guest house when I was seventeen, and after many sleepless nights suffering from intense humidity, heat, and a relentless allergy, I conceded that perhaps God, after all, had other plans for me. Mother Mary Catherine agreed with me, but she also challenged me with what was to me a terrifying possibility.

The first time I visited her in the convent parlor was an occasion I'll never forget. This parlor was tiny compared to the one in the Precious Blood Monastery, for this contemplative community of Episcopal women was much smaller than the Roman Catholic community I had known in Portland. Instead of whitewash, the room's immediate sensory image was that of warm woodwork and patterned upholstered chairs. There was a grille, as with all enclosed orders in those days, but it consisted of well-spaced vertical beams of naturally stained thin wooden beams, rather than the closed lattice work arrangement I had seen before. Mother Mary Catherine sat on the other side of the grille, sometimes leaning her arms on the table-like ledge where the wooden beams stopped about three feet from the floor.

47

She began our conversation by telling me of her own religious vocation. It came to her in a rather dramatic way. When she was quite a young woman, she discovered that she had cancer of the nose. Believing her life to be in danger, the doctors gave her little to hope for. But her faith was strong. She left a physician's office in prayer one day. "God, if you permit me to live, I will give my whole life entirely to you." It was some time after that when the medical prognosis changed. Her doctors told her that the cancer could probably be contained. She became a Poor Clare nun, fulfilling her promise in this way in deepest gratitude to God. Her life had been spared, but her physical suffering was to continue throughout her life, as containing the disease involved (and I understand still does involve) repeated surgeries from year to year. I did not meet a woman wracked with pain that day, though her body has surely endured more than I could ever bear. I met instead a sensitive, down-to-earth woman of God, a woman of prayer and humor, good sense and great courage. Though her face bore the marks of her illness, I saw in it only radiance and peace, the beauty of one who understands life from the inside out, and who loves it all.

Being moved by her story and even more by her presence, I heard what she had to say to me about my own vocation as if it were the voice of God speaking to me. These are the words she spoke to me: "If God has spoken to you through the spirituality of the Carmelite saints—as indeed God has—then perhaps you are to be a Carmelite, despite the obvious hindrances. If this is so, there is no point in your trying to be a Poor Clare, for a genuine vocation can never be compromised. If God intends for you to be something, you must discover a way of becoming it. If God intends for you to be a Carmelite, you must be a Carmelite, even if the only way for this to happen, given your circumstances, is for you to found an Anglican Order of Carmelites."

I was terribly frightened, for there was truth in what she

said, and there was a suggestion of struggle and effort and even sacrifice that I was not eager to undertake. Though the immediate context of a possible calling to become a Carmelite changed, the basic sense of what Mother Mary Catherine had to say about a vocation stood true. It was for me now to test the exact nature of my religious vocation. Her words carried me out the door and on through the next few years, and as a matter of fact they are carrying me still. My initial response has also not changed much through the years. I am no more brave now than I was then.

I left Long Island with a cautious heart. "And I thought my calling was so simple," I said to myself—and to God.

My family was much relieved when I came home to Oregon with no further notions of shutting myself away from them as a Poor Clare. What I had to tell them after that did not offer them further comfort, however. What in the world would their daughter come up with next?

I began to revise my idea of the future. For four years I had remained firm, against the better judgment of nearly everyone, in my resolve to become a contemplative religious. I had translated my sense of calling into these terms because it was the only way I knew for a woman to give herself completely to God. From an early age I had experienced a deep inclination to give my life totally to a God who had clearly called me to do that. It was a compelling inner imperative and I knew no other way of responding to it than by entering a religious order—and a contemplative one at that, one which emphasized silence and solitude as did the Order of Carmelites. It's interesting to me now when I recall how much I identified with St. Thérèse of Lisieux to note that she expressed an unrealized vocation to the priesthood, but she became a Carmelite nun instead, devoting herself to praying for priests since she could not become one. She died early, no doubt of frustration.

As a matter of fact, too many generations of religious women have probably died of frustration—the unsatisfying substitution of one life's commitment for another that was more pressing but seemed impossible. I suppose that their situation was little different from that of resigned married women who died spent and old in their youth, women who knew no recourse other than to burn themselves out in child-bearing and rearing and as domestic laborers, while some latent genius in them may have gone untapped until it, too, died. I am not speaking of all Sisters in religious orders or of all married women, for many women certainly have genuine vocations to marriage or religious life, just as many men do. But it's one thing to choose these possibilities as areas of self-commitment and another to submit to them because there seems no hope of realizing one's real desires. (The Liberation Movement stands for choice over submission, but there is nevertheless a *surrender* in the choice. While choice alone can become fanaticism and submission alone can become lukewarmness, choice and surrender together form commitment and its consequent self-transcendence and self-realization.)

Mother Mary Catherine had given me plenty to think about. I wasn't completely clear on what I was to do, so after several months of prayer for guidance and courage, I went to see an acquaintance, Monsignor Thomas Tobin, whom I had come to know through mutual Roman Catholic friends. He was the pastor of a Roman Catholic parish in Portland, and at that time he was also a liturgical expert at the Vatican Council II in Rome.

When I went to see Tom Tobin, I had an ecumenical proposal in mind. In the 1830's, when religious orders began to sprout in the Church of England, it was common for Anglican women and men to spend some time in Roman Catholic convents or monasteries to gain experiential understanding of religious life. Then these women and men would form

Anglican religious orders often modelled after the Roman Catholic communities. Since I happened to be living in the age of ecumenism, it seemed highly fitting to add an ecumenical dimension to my religious orientation, so I suggested to Monsignor Tobin that I be given permission by Rome to live in a Carmelite community as an Anglican guest to learn about the style and spirit of that Order from the inside. This would be preparation for the foundation of an Episcopal Order of Carmelites. With his typical enthusiasm he responded, "Good idea! We'll get you the permission you need. Write a letter explaining the plan and I'll deliver it in person to the head of the Sacred Congregation for Religious when I'm in Rome for the Council next month."

The Secretary of the Sacred Congregation for Religious was a suave French Dominican religious, and an archbishop who would soon become a cardinal. In the spring of 1965, a trilingual correspondence was initiated, with letters crossing the Atlantic by post and personal courier, among Archbishop Philippe, his secretary, Monsignor Tobin and myself, in French, Italian, and English. Things were still up in the air when, in August that year, I went on a long trip abroad with my mother.

For several months, mother and I visited relatives who had left Russia to settle in Germany. Each of us had interests outside of Germany. I had friends in Rome to look up. Mother was doing research for a biography of Archduke Otto, last of the Austrian Hapsburgs, who had commissioned it during an earlier visit to Austria. We had taken a thirty-day break from these contacts to tour Europe. Near the beginning of our tour we were sightseeing at the German castle, Schloss Solitude, near Stuggart, when we met another American. He was Jim LaChapelle, a priest from Texas studying in Rome and staying at the motherhouse of his religious order. We took down his address and promised to look him up when our trip took us to Rome later on.

51

About ten days after Stuttgart, Jim was giving us a personalized tour of the Eternal City. "We have to go to St. Peter's Square at noon so you can see the colorful display of cardinals coming out for their lunch break," he informed us the first morning. And a colorful display it was. I had my camera poised to capture a moment of the pageantry as rich reds and purples poured into the piazza and men with peculiar hats ambled out for noon refreshment. Suddenly, looking down into the lens of my camera, I saw a familiar face and form. There, in a plain black cassock, in startling contrast to the plumage around him, was my friend from Oregon, Tom Tobin. He spotted me at the same time. Neither of us had known that the other one was in Rome. I was aware that he went off occasionally to participate in the Council, but I never knew exactly when he'd be in Rome and when he'd be at home.

"Excellent," was his quick greeting to me, removing his fried egg hat politely and reaching for my hand. "You can talk with Archbishop Philippe yourself. I was just going to see him about you." Next thing I knew I was running to keep up with his stride, praying that my hand would remain attached to the rest of me as it was being transported across the ancient square inside Monsignor Tobin's tight grip. I could barely keep up with myself as we went flying past Swiss Guards who had no time to blink as the sixty-year-old Monsignor waved his Vatican pass before their eyes, then gliding up flights of stairs, my feet touching down every fourth step, and finally into the atrium of the inner chamber of a prince of the Roman Catholic Church. My friend matter-of-factly sat me down and then as quickly as he'd gotten me there he left me—to find Archbishop Philippe, he said, and hasten him up to his own office, lunchtime or not, as expeditiously as he'd done with me.

Meanwhile, my mother had discovered a Russian prelate in the crowd and was manuevering her way over to the ecumenical headquarters so that she could engage in conversation with someone in her mother tongue. Our guide by now was sufficiently bewildered by this now-you-see-them-now-you-don't activity, his two tourists rushing in four directions. Amazingly, he did manage to catch up with both of us, and even to bring us together again. He was an agile person with some experience of Vatican ways.

When Archbishop Philippe arrived he found me and two Italian religious waiting for him, all nervously saying our prayers. He addressed the others briefly in Italian and they left. Then he addressed me in formal English. I told him my name and mentioned my proposal. At the magic word "ecumenical" his face lit up and with a gracious gesture he ushered me into his office. In that Rococo room he lavished me with blessings and approbation. At the end of our interview I was given official letters of endorsement with the seal of the Sacred Congregation for Religious.

Thus ends the fairy tale part of that adventure. I had to go home and face a few realities.

In late November, mother and I sailed from Bremerhaven to New York on the final voyage of the *S.S. United States.* Early in December I began writing letters of application to various Carmelite monasteries with copies of the Vatican documents to add strength to my proposal. Even though the final days of the ecumenical Council in Rome were approaching, there were still corners of Christendom that remained little touched by its influence. The enclosed, conservative women of the Order of Discalced Carmelites had not yet opened their doors to the renewing winds of the ecumenical era. I continued to knock on those doors relentlessly, becoming for some persons a rather annoying ecumenical movement of one. In twelve months I had applied to twelve monasteries and been refused a dozen times. I called it the Year of the Great Rejection. Combined with the letters of rejection from religious communities were the many less personal rejection slips of my first year's efforts to be a published poet—though there were at least occasional acceptances from the editors.

Through that year it was becoming apparent to me that my calling was *to wait*. I began slowly to outgrow my youthful impatience. I came to perceive in myself strength and endurance that was more than mere patience, or even mere persistence. And I came to value the wisdom and friendship of a person I've already told you a little about, my teacher and confidante and sister in Christ, Rosaire.

Our relationship was deepening. It had become a source of energy and creativity for me. The love we came to have for each other and the sharing we experienced together in prayer and conversation formed a power that extended beyond ourselves.

I had already realized this kind of power in my relationship with Pauline, and in different ways with Barnabas and Mary. It is a power of love that I have come to value above everything else on earth, a power so strong that nothing can break or weaken it. I have experienced it not only in individual relationships, but more recently within communities of women, as the experience of sisterly love grows up among us as we bring our griefs, longings, hopes, fears, frustrations, bleeding wounds and open joys to one another. It is the power of entrusting oneself fully to another human being, or to a community of human beings, but it's more than this.

When such a bond forms between or among persons, it takes the shape of creative energy that gives value and intensity to all the dynamics within the relationship. It becomes a bond of intimacy that includes healing and celebration. Love of this kind is holistic—the whole-making power in human relationships.

I believe that this kind of love, the love of true friendship, has a creativity and a fruition of its own, and that it gives life beyond itself as truly as erotic love. The love between or among friends can conceive and bear into being dreams and

54

visions that transcend the relationship and live independently of those who dreamed them—but not independently of the power of love that called them forth into reality. As erotic love between a woman and man has the power to call forth new life, *agapé,* the love of genuine friendship, has the power to create out of shared dreams and desires something that can be of lasting value for the human community.

Sister Rosaire and I experienced our relationship as a growing gift that we treasured. The creativity in it came forth in the form of a dream. We had begun to share a ministry together, as well as to pray together. As we carried on a joint counseling program at a local neighborhood center and arranged for high school students to make visits to nearby nursing homes, we drew such joy from our work together that one day it occurred to us to share it with others. I should say that it occurred to Rosaire.

We had been doing these kinds of things together for about eight months, and we had come to experience prayer between us as the connective power in the universe. My situation with the Carmelites was becoming less and less promising. But the kind of contemplative ecumenism that I felt called to was something that Sister Rosaire and I were experiencing together in fact.

Sister Rosaire said to me one evening, "I think that what we're doing is something we need to share with others. I think that we're unwittingly on the verge of something more important than just the two of us. I don't know what it is yet, but I feel it, and I believe we should pray about it."

My inner response to this was similar to what I felt during Mother Mary Catherine's last conversation with me. A kind of visceral wilting, a sense of spinal disintegration. With a kind of helpless groan that meant, "O God, now what?" I just said, "All right. We'll pray about it." Secretly I was hoping that God had other things to do than to attend to these particular prayers. Praying was the least and the most I felt I could do at the time.

Ecumenical Oblates

When I was in Rome in 1965, I spent some time with friends at the International Center for the Movement for a Better World—*Mondo Migliore*. It was a modern place about forty miles south of Rome via the Appian Way, near Rocco di Papa and the Pope's summer residence at Castel Gondolfo. People had come there from all over the world to go through one of the many programs of Christian renewal. I met Thomas from India, a man in his thirties who had dedicated himself to working among India's poor, the ill, and the dying, joining himself to the ministry of Mother Teresa. I met Matthew, a priest from Kenya who one day slipped a present into my hand—an Easter egg wrapped in a cloth that had held the First Communion wafer of his African niece. Others were there from all parts of the globe. But since I had only a few days on that first occasion, I made only brief contact with the many interesting people at *Mondo Migliore*.

The Better World Movement began in the thirties, when a simple Italian priest named Lombardi began to preach publicly against facism, a Christian soapbox response to Mussolini. After World War II, the Movement went through a process of adaptation to the changing world situation as it interfaced with Christian and non-Christian peoples in Third World countries.

In the sixties, the Better World Movement focused on developing a Christian statement against the unChrist-like imposition of economic imperialism and political oppression of any kind throughout the world, especially in underdeveloped and so-called non-democratic countries. It existed as an extraordinary kind of mission that could separate the Christian message from Western culture; it thereby valued and honored the cultural integrity of indigenous peoples across the hemispheres.

The people I encountered in early autumn of 1965 at *Mondo Migliore* represented Christian communities in Ceylon, South India, New Zealand, Malaysia, the African nations, the Pacific islands, South and Central American countries, the British Isles, Canada, and the United States. In a short time my life became immeasurably enriched by the slight contact I had with persons whose perspective and place on the earth were so different from my own.

The following spring back in Oregon I learned that there was to be a Better World Conference at my own retreat center, Our Lady of Peace (Roman Catholic) in Beaverton. It was scheduled for Easter week. I signed up right away, and was delighted to find that the five persons coming to conduct the conference were among those I'd met in Rome months earlier. I was the only non-Roman Catholic at the conference, but I was welcomed with grace and warmth, as has so often been my experience in similar circumstances.

On the final day of the conference there was a special Mass for Christian Unity. It was particularly moving to me because it was the first time that I'd received communion with that community, for I had refrained from taking communion during the week to avoid offending anyone. By the end of the week a community spirit had developed within the group. The thought of not sharing the Bread of Life with everyone else at our final Eucharist seemed unthinkable to me. The presiding priest agreed that it would be highly inap-

57

propriate for me not to take communion with the rest of the community. (In case any question was raised—which didn't happen—we could claim "legality" on the basis of my Orthodox chrismation, since the Roman Church was then more amenable to "emergency" intercommunion with the Orthodox Church, but no other: Games Christians Play.)

It was like ending a week's fast when I finally broke bread with everyone else. I felt tremendous inner energy after the Eucharist for Christian Unity. There was opportunity for some free time alone before lunch, so I went back to my room and yielded to an overwhelming urge to write. For an hour I wrote at white heat.

I was reflecting on the implications of my experience at the liturgy. We had offered the Eucharist for unity, not a unity of conformity, but of common commitment to Christ. In my mind, this unity was not organizational, did not require persons to bend themselves into a pre-fab mold of Christian life, but was rather a unity of mutuality experienced through the integrity of our very differences. In other words, organic unity rather than organizational unity meant the actual celebration, never the dissolution, of our uniqueness. The sharing of diversity, not the sharing of sameness, is what enriches human community. For me, worship and prayer are the very heart of ecumenism, but worship and prayer would quickly go sterile if all the branches of Christendom were to surrender their particular traditions in a misguided effort to achieve uniformity. Variety really is the salt and substance of life.

I was thinking that the differences we've allowed to divide us as Christians and as human beings are the very gifts we have to offer one another. Without them, there is nothing special about any of us, nothing attractive, magnetic, appealing, alive. We've twisted our various charisms into tools of competition in the Christian Olympics: those with greatest endurance win the prize of orthodoxy for their denomination. Applying Rollo May's definitions, we've substituted competitive power for integrative power: acting against each other when we could have been acting with each other. Thoughts similar to these were flying through my mind as I wrote that morning. Finally, it seemed to be all out on paper. I stopped writing and took a look at results. It was a little like automatic writing, for the words came from the integrative part of my own psyche, a part not wholly conscious or deliberate. What I saw in my hands was a paper headed "Schema for the Community of Christian At-onement." (It became, in one of its later revisions, the Rule for the Ecumenical Oblates.) I had a suspicion that this had something to do with all that praying Sister Rosaire and I had undertaken through the preceding four months.

On the chance that this was so, I did the only sensible thing: gave the whole thing back to God. I went into the chapel with the "schema," took it up to the altar steps, and said, "I don't know what this is all about, but if you have something to do with it, you'd better take over from here on out."

The following afternoon I took it over to Sister Rosaire, hoping that she'd have an idea on what we should do about it. She said, "Yes, this is surely the answer to our prayer. Now we'll live by the Rule for a year, then go to our bishops for official sanction for others to join us." That, it appeared, was that. I was, and continue to be, completely startled by the whole thing.[1]

---

[1] Here is the Rule of what is now called the Ecumenical Oblates, with a portion of the current re-visioning of our Constitution-in-process:

Love one another.
Receive everyone as Christ.
Pray always.

... Ecumenical Oblates form a spiritual community living under one Rule [but not necessarily one roof], and with the common purpose of overcoming denominational barriers through prayer and mutual sharing of God's gifts to us in many different forms.

The center of the community is Christ, the Creative Word of God,

I did not have grandiose notions about our dream, especially now that it seemed on the verge of becoming a reality. In fact, I was quite bewildered by my own part in it and by the apparent double direction of my own life. I deferred to

---

speaking the eternally New Speech into our lives. We are equal members in our relationship to each other because we are one in the Word of God, we share one baptism in Christ.

Our community is a unity of persons who are aware of the inherent unity of the Church and who seek to realize it more and more, and to make it apparent to others. Our unity does not consist in uniformity but in spiritual communion that is the result of a common life in God, achieved in encounter with the one Christ in prayer, and in human encounter with one another.

Our community is a community in process, a place of personal friendship and companionship in Christ for persons responding to God's call to an ecumenical, contemplative, and apostolic life. It enriches these ministries by increasing the spiritual community of Christians who might otherwise feel isolated in their calling.

The community's motivating spirit of unity in diversity draws us into union with God through prayer, union with the world through the servanthood of Christ, union with one another in the Spirit.

. . . Each person is free to discover and develop her or his own spirituality and unique ministry. Intimacy with God in the joy, simplicity, and availability of Christ is a gift that each person receives in a special way. This personal, unique relationship with God and the community will form the basis for the individual's special offering as an Ecumenical Oblate. [Oblates make the same corporate commitment but later on make unique personal vows. The only restriction upon liturgical life and general witness is that we use non-exclusive, non-sexist language, and are sensitive to standing against sexism, racism, and classism in our own participation in Church and society: the restriction becomes an expansion.]

[The words *Ecumenical* and *Oblate*] are used in their etymological sense. *Ecumenical* means world-embracing and implies an open-hearted attitude toward life and persons. *Oblate* is not associated with its occasional use in reference to one who is peripherally connected with a religious community. Here the Oblates are the religious community. They are simply persons who *offer* themselves—make oblations of themselves in union with Christ, for the realization of the intrinsic unity among all Christian and all human persons, and in harmony with all creation. The Ecumenical Oblate holds the world close with open arms, recognizing, celebrating, and offering back to God the holiness of all that is. This is the meaning of the offering of love of an Ecumenical Oblate.

60

Sister Rosaire's sense of purpose even though I had personal reservations about launching out on totally uncharted ecumenical waters. We seemed to be engaged in founding an ecumenical religious community. I thought that I was supposed to be a Carmelite, and I was confused by this development. But one thing was obvious. This was real. It was happening, which was more than I could say about my becoming a Carmelite. Once again I had to surrender to reality. I wondered why life seemed to be getting more complicated all the time. "God," I prayed, "is it always going to be like this?"

And then something happened that left me in complete despair.

My friend Sister Rosaire had been feeling tired and run-down all winter that year. In the spring, just after we had decided to begin living by our new Rule, she began to have frequent colds and flu attacks, never really getting over one bout before another would take her. The other Sisters were worried about her, and so was I. But none of us thought anything was seriously wrong. She had arranged to spend summer in the motherhouse of her order in Mission San Jose, California, where the warm southern air could help her recover. I planned to meet her in San Francisco three weeks after she left Portland, which would have been in mid-July.

About ten days after she left, I went to my mother's house one afternoon for a visit. As soon as I walked in the door, I knew something was terribly wrong. My mother was afraid to look at me. The only other time I had seen her like this was when I was six years old and she had to tell me that a treasured pet of mine had died.

"What is it?" I asked. "What's wrong?"

Then she said it, still not facing me. "Your friend Sister Rosaire is dead."

I felt like someone had removed the veins from my body. Stunned, disbelieving, I stammered out some incoherent questions. "How do you know? How did it happen?

Where was she?"

The Mother General had called my mother's house and had left the news with mother when she couldn't reach me. Mother Mary Dominic's report to my mother was that Sister Rosaire had been ill at the motherhouse with another cold, but that the cold developed into pneumonia. She was taken to the hospital where a tracheostomy had been performed on her to enable her to breathe. During this surgical procedure, the physicians discovered that she had erythmatous lupus, a disease whose effect is like a tuberculosis of the blood vessels. She never regained consciousness. Her own blood sister, a nursing nun in another order, came to be with her and care for her. In only five days, she was dead.

This information was more than I could bear. I went into the basement of my mother's house and all the together places of my body and soul came apart. It was more than two hours before mother could talk to me again. She had never seen me grieve like that. Later she said the walls of her house shook with my sobs.

Losing Sister Rosaire was the first major loss of my life. I went to her funeral in Mission San Jose. The other Dominican Sisters were sensitive to me and to the relationship that Rosaire and I had. I was left to pray alone beside her unbreathing body for as long a time as I wanted. I met her own blood sister who nursed her and was with her when she died, and it gave me peace to hear that Rosaire knew no pain in the end. Her other brothers and sisters were there, talking about her as "Mimi," her family nickname, and I thought how like her all her siblings were—warm, gracious, charming, outgoing, sensitive. I was glad to know them, for it made her presence even fuller than before to me.

It was many months before my sorrow began to diminish, before I could sense once again the bond that was still unbroken between us. I began to have an inkling that Rosaire was very much present to me, that her love could span the barrier of death. Often I still have moments when I know that she is around, twinkling at me, enjoying something with me, and the fact that her self-expression is now non-physical makes it no less real to me. She herself is "eastering" in her own unique way in God's eternity.

We had barely begun, that spring, to live out the plan that Rosaire had suggested for us, of living our Rule together for a year before going to our bishops for their blessing and recognition. Now my friend and sister was gone. I was alone. I had no idea how to live out a Rule for an ecumenical community all by myself. In a way I felt that, not Sister Rosaire, but God had abandoned me, by taking her from me. I knew only two things to do. The first was to pray. The second was to wait.

I waited for more than six months, without guidance from any living soul, until I could bear it no longer. Sometime the following winter I went back to Monsignor Tobin with my confusion and deep sense of loss.

With all the Vatican papers in the world I had not been able to find a Carmelite monastery on this continent that would accept me as an ecumenical guest. Meanwhile, another kind of direction was forming simultaneously with my growing commitment to ecumenism. But my guide and cherished companion in the new direction was now dead. Cut off from her illuminating thought and judgment I felt inert. What should I do?

Tom Tobin's bright, deliberate voice was the first clear thing I had heard in months. "We'll go back to Archbishop Philippe after you see your bishop. This idea is better than the Carmelite proposal."

By now the Vatican Council had ended, and the "we" in Monsignor Tobin's suggestion proved to be editorial. This time I found myself alone in Rome. The money that my father had saved for my now defunct college education and my own savings from a year's employment as a registered medical secretary at one of the St. Jude's Homes combined to get me to Europe for the second time in 1967. I began my pilgrimage by making a visit to *Mondo Migliore,* this time as a full participant in a month-long training program with people as inspiring to be with as those I'd met there before. When the month was over I had to deal with the two overlapping plans in my mind. I still had no way of getting them together, or of resolving their apparent conflicting directions.

My first intention was to try to settle my relationship one way or another with the Roman Catholic Carmelites. I took a bus to the Teresianum, the Mother House of the entire Carmelite Order, both women and men. It was my good luck that the General Chapter (a kind of monastic convention) was in session, and Carmelites were there from all over the world.

After several false starts with an Italian and then an English Carmelite, I finally made contact with an American named Christopher Latimer, who was a Provincial (regional advisor) for monasteries in northeastern United States. Since that meeting in Rome ten years ago I've heard from him two or three times, though we have not seen one another again. My recollection of him is that of a man with sharp intuition and good sense, the latter being not a common enough trait among religious persons. After hearing my story with an earnest ear, he gave me the names and addresses of two Carmelite monasteries for women in New England. He told me that the superiors of these communities were both women of great wisdom and human warmth, and that they were bright, informed, and "with it"—with the spirit of the times. This was a revelation to me, and it renewed my faith in the validity of my own pilgrim's process.

After I left the Teresianum, I went back into Vatican City to see Archbishop Philippe again, this time with new business. I explained to him my former frustrations with the

Carmelites, and also how Sister Rosaire and I had come upon a new idea and model for contemporary ecumenical religious life that was similar to the Taizé community, but for married and single women and men, not just celibate males. Archbishop Philippe sent me to Cardinal Bea, saying that this was "a most wonderful idea," but it was more properly in the jurisdiction of the Secretariat for Christian Unity.

I had no magic passes and no Tom Tobin this time, and my friend Jim LaChapelle, the young American priest who was formerly our guide, was no longer in Rome. I was completely on my own, and I had to be my own diplomat in Vatican City. I obtained a pass to one of Pope Paul's private Masses, but I was only a slight woman alone in a crowd. This time I had to be ingenious, quick, and lithe enough on my own to make the necessary contacts, a feat that involved considerably more physical skill than had been required of me before. I recall getting past the watchful eye and quick wrists of the Swiss Guard and climbing over a wooden barricade, being hoisted from behind by a Spanish Franciscan and pulled from ahead by a Belgian Jesuit. After a brief visit with Archbishop Philippe I went down the street and around the corner to a square building appropriately on the edge of Vatican City, the Secretariat for Christian Unity.

Cardinal Bea was ill, and in his absence I was received, somewhat coolly, by the British chairman of the Roman Catholic side of the Anglican-Roman Catholic Consultation. This tall, grey, distinguished looking Englishman was neither as warm nor as enthusiastic as the French Archbishop had been. My first impression was that his thin, concentrated posture conveyed equal messages of precision and suspicion. After twenty minutes of conversation, it occurred to me that his reservation and caution were probably characteristic. This man was not one to give overt encouragement to anybody, I thought, and perhaps a gesture of forthright—if impersonal—interest from him was as valuable as the generous support I'd received from the Frenchman.

"You do not need official papers from us," he said. "You have our prayers and our good wishes and hopes for vocations to an ecumenical religious life. If God wills it, such an ecumenical community will take shape. But it may take many years. You, and we, must be patient." With this positive last word from him, I left Rome and flew to London to attend the Anglican Conference on Religious Life at Oxford, and to tour England with my father and Brother Andrew who would be attending the Conference representing the Society of St. Paul.

I arrived at Heathrow Airport in the middle of the afternoon on a Friday in August of 1967. While waiting in downtown Rome for the airport bus I'd gotten hungry, and went into a pizzeria across the street from Santa Maria Maggiore. When I ordered half a small pizza to go, a robust Italian woman cut a large slab of the house specialty and proceeded to wrap it up in what looked exactly like American gift wrap, complete with colored string. I was so fascinated with the aesthetic wrapping that I decided to save my lunch to show my father and Brother Andrew, who could also help me eat the huge portion. It was only as I was going through British customs at Heathrow that it dawned on me that the warm pizza under my arm might be an illegal entry. But no one asked me if I had any pizza with me. "I see you've got that nice birthday gift, Mum. Anything else you bought in Italy?" No, that was all. We ate smuggled pizza all the way to Oxford, the Volkswagen minibus positively reeking of the released odors of pepperoni and cheese.

The Anglican Conference on Religious Life lasted for three days and consisted of lectures and workshops on different aspects of religious life. Representatives of hundreds of Anglican religious orders from all over the world were in attendance, all in traditional religious garb. I felt surrounded by anachronisms.

Roman Catholic religious by 1967 were beginning to let go of medieval paraphernalia in dress and custom, but Anglican religious were clinging to the past as if they were the sole preservers of true monastic tradition in the Western Church. I have to admit that, criticisms aside, I was enchanted at tea time to find myself in the charming garden where Charles Dodgson wrote *Alice in Wonderland,* surrounded by people wearing clothes from another century. In that atmosphere I fully expected to see the White Rabbit jump out at any moment to dangle his watch in front of the peculiar crowd.

The conference was a good experience in many ways. It deepened my understanding of the history and spirituality of my own theological tradition, and it intensified my recognition of the human trait of resistance to change. In the face of radical renewal encroaching upon the Church, here were individuals struggling with the pain born out of abandonment of old and familiar things, not quite willing to adapt themselves to the unfamiliar and new. The high price of growth was apparent to all, and each small group grappled with it differently through those three days.

Episcopalians in the United States had only just received the first of a lengthy series of trial liturgies designed to replace the 1928 version of the Book of Common Prayer, a version only slightly different from the 1662 edition. There was an interesting pattern to these trial liturgies. Their language, it seemed to me, reflected sensitivity to people's fear of change on the part of the Standing Liturgical Commission that drafted them. In the trial liturgy of 1967, the pronouns referring to people were made contemporary, but the pronouns referring to God were left untouched from their sixteenth century *thee/thou* mode. The rational response to the linguistic inconsistency was that human beings were treated as real people in a real 20th-century frame of reference, but God was still treated as an Elizabethan English gentleman.

Perhaps the Standing Liturgical Commission was willing to give people time to get used to the idea of contemporary language before hitting them with changes in the most sensitive spot—that of liturgical God-language. In the 1970 trial liturgy, God was removed from the time warp and brought into the 20th century with the rest of us. I am hoping for a similar pattern in the eradication of sexist language from the final authorized edition; at present the people-language has been freed of gender bias but God-language remains one-sidedly male. It will be well for this to be changed so that we can actually use the new Book of Common Prayer. The point of these revisions of our prayer book is to re-authenticate the language and theology of our worship so that we say what we mean when we pray together. If we no longer mean that God is male and women are not part of God's people, our worship needs to reflect this belief. Language can be a source of attitude adjustment, and words can help us to mean what we say when we speak of our relationship to God and each other. Language both reflects and reinforces human attitudes, which is why it's such a sensitive issue.

Restoring integrity to worship requires tremendous giving and courage by all, for it involves changes at a deep level of our corporate life. The process exposes our weaknesses and our unwholeness and forces us to stretch and heal ourselves. Change is never easy, and the more radical the change—the more it touches our roots—the more painful it is. Nearly every organism under the sun has an approach/avoidance response to change, even the inevitable change accompanying natural growth and maturation. Nothing is more traumatic than the life process itself, because life is a constant opening into transitions, and there is never opportunity to get used to this particular state of being: we are too busily *becoming* for that.

The Oxford Conference was a symbol to me of the approach/avoidance response that church people in particular exhibit in the face of change. The upheaval that Episcopalians and other church members have been undergoing for the past fifteen or so years is an intense effort to emerge as honest-to-God 20th-century Christians, able to acknowledge and respond to the needs of the world authentically in our own times, making the Gospel a reality in our lives. The Church needs to be pulled into the 20th century with its integrity restored and intact. In England I learned that whatever course my vocation finally was to take, I had to be part of this pull.

When the Oxford Conference and our travels around England were over, I flew from London to Montreal, and then to Ottawa, Ontario, where I took a bus up into the northern wilderness area to visit the Madonna House Apostolate training center in Combermere.

In 1966, I had made friends with Mary Kay Rowland, the director of Stella Maris House, a branch of the Madonna House Apostolate in Portland. Mary Kay and I had spent several weekends together at the beach, praying and being quiet together, and we had come to find in one another sources of strength and encouragement through the ups and downs of our efforts to serve God and people gracefully. We were drawn to each other through a shared appreciation of Russian and contemplative spirituality.

The Madonna House Apostolate is a Roman Catholic community of lay women and men and priests founded by Catherine de Hueck Doherty, a Russian woman of my mother's generation. The Apostolate itself is an extension of Catherine's blending of deep Eastern spirituality with Western culture. In the various houses of the Apostolate throughout the world, many Russian folk traditions are observed in liturgy and community life, particularly around Christmas and Easter. Stella Maris House was the only place outside the Russian community and my mother's kitchen where I found the traditional Russian Easter foods I described earlier. I used to love to pray with the small Stella Maris community in their simple chapel, where the Eucharist and the daily offices were enhanced with Byzantine prayers, and icons graced the corners of the room.

Mary Kay had encouraged me to visit Madonna House itself, and to experience Catherine at first hand. At the end of this summer pilgrimage, it was possible for me to do so.

My first impression of Catherine reminded me of the pictures I had seen of her friend Dorothy Day: an aging woman of amazing robustness and strength—more than strength: actual physical power, coming from an inner steadfastness of purpose and conviction. Her hair was combed back and pinned to her head, framing her rugged face, a face almost peasant-like, slightly squared, full, and ruddy. Her deep eyes had the penetrating power described by those who have known medicine men and healing women, Indian shamans or Russian staretzes. She sat at the head of the table where I took my first meal at Madonna House during my week's visit. Her manner was matriarchal, always teaching, reflecting, expressing, speaking forth her inner processes for the benefit of the community. She was discussing some theological question with a young visitor, speaking with great animation and intensity. I don't recall what she said, but the vitality of her manner is a vivid memory. What I heard Norman Cousins say of Buckminster Fuller in a radio interview recently also applies to her: it doesn't matter whether or not you understand what she says, for she gives what others cannot by putting you in touch with the eternal, by moving you into a deeper sensitivity to life itself.

I was moved by Catherine, by her unique and powerful spirituality, at once child-like and commanding, and by her humanity, spontaneously expressing itself through the real feelings and experiences of a particular moment, with a particular person.

I was especially impressed by her generosity of time and energy (she made it a point to speak to each of the hundreds of visitors who poured through Madonna House during the summer) and by the spirit of ecumenism that she lived out within her community. She perceived herself as a link between East and West, bringing to the Apostolate her own outpouring of Russian custom and theology—an incarnational, iconic theology of contemplative prayer turned into the action of service to the poor and suffering. Besides the work of the Apostolate in responding to the physical needs of the world's hungry, its greatest gift to the world is a uniquely Russian response to spiritual hunger, something called *poustinia*, which Catherine is responsible for bringing to North America.

In the Russian language, *poustinia* means *desert*. It describes metaphorically a place where one can go to be alone with God. In Russia, this place has traditionally been a hermitage, a simple hut or cabin in the woods. For contemporary Western people, it can mean one room of a house reserved for prayer and contemplation in the midst of the city or suburbs. The *poustinia* is a place of centering. Its characteristics are simplicity, silence, and solitude, usually accompanied by fasting on tea and bread, and the study of only one book— Holy Scriptures. The solitude of the *poustinia* isn't interpreted as strict isolation, for the traditional Russian *poustinikki* were holy women and men who provided hospitality of the heart to pilgrims, sharing with travellers what they had to offer in spiritual food and physical comfort.

At Madonna House, I found American and Canadian Roman Catholics engaged in the *poustinia* experience. There were several small *poustinias* in the woods where members of the community could go to spend twenty-four hours or more alone in prayer. Some members of the Apostolate lived in the *poustinia,* working out a rhythm of solitary prayer for three days a week and community life the remaining four

71

when they would return to the Center and live among the others, sharing the overflow of their prayerful solitude. I was impressed with the possibilities for creative incorporation of the individual rhythms while relating them to the larger community in various ways. The presence of the *poustinia* seemed to be a source of spiritual gifts for the whole community, balancing the very active side of the apostolic ministry. It seemed to me that the *poustinia*, a hidden gem in my own Russian heritage, could become uniquely adapted to American spirituality. American spirituality is eclectic, like our ethnically mixed country, and it includes richness through a variety of disciplines and modalities.

Catherine expanded my notions of contemplative ecumenism. While I was at Combermere I made a *poustinia* experience myself, going into a small square building in the middle of a field at the end of a dirt road for two days. It was called the House of Gold. I learned to appreciate the *poustinia* concept, and it has since been adapted to our own community's needs. One of our Brothers today is a full time *poustinik* in the Wisconsin wilderness, providing a place for others to have that experience as well. My own rhythm has developed into a daily *poustinia* of time, rather than place: I need four hours a day of contemplative solitude, which I usually take in the middle of the night when I can be sure that the telephone will sleep.

In Combermere that summer I felt that I'd come full circle, for the contemplative side of a life of consecration that had attracted me to Carmel was incorporated into the daily routines of outer-directed ministry through this very Russian form of the *poustinia*. It was a gift to me of my own inheritance, not coming to me through my own mother, but through the maternal wisdom of this other Russian woman in an unexpected place, and in a remarkable way.

Still, I had the whole question of my future and relationship with the Carmelites to resolve. On the last lap of my quest that summer, I left Madonna House to visit one of the New England Carmelite monasteries I'd heard about from Father Christopher Latimer in Rome.

One mild, balmy August morning, I rang the door bell at the Carmel of Barrington, Rhode Island, and was welcomed inside by a bright-looking middle-aged extern Sister. The nuns were expecting me, since I had written ahead to be sure that a visit would be convenient. The extern Sister showed me to the chapel, which was extraordinarily beautiful, modern and spacious and open, filled with daylight, a truly sacred space. Then she took me into the Sisters' parlor and told me that Mother Mary Cyril would be there in just a moment. I was excited more than apprehensive, for I had an intuition that this Carmel really *was* different, a feeling I probably received from the atmosphere of the chapel.

One look at Mother Cyril as she entered the room from the Sisters' side of the parlor, and I felt sure that my intuition was right. Her broad smile, her weloming, alert, and interested eyes told me that I would not be dismissed without being heard. In fact, Mother Cyril received me with a warmth and graciousness that were entirely beyond my experience before or since our meeting. She, too, was a woman of my mother's generation, somewhat older than my own mother, but so alive and youthful in her manner that she seemed to have more energy and zest for life than most people I knew in their twenties.

Her eyes were windows of expressiveness and feeling as she listened to my story. Through the reflection of her glasses I saw worlds of understanding and deep recognition in them. My joy and relief were so great, finding in this woman someone who appeared to know what my heart's desire was, who took it seriously, who echoed back to me the loving desires for God within her own heart. By the end of several hours we were practically dancing together—and would have been if the old-style grille weren't between us. At one point

73

Mother Cyril went out to call all the Sisters together to meet me, and the parlor became filled with the whole community, each Sister seeming to have some of the same lively, loving spirit shining forth from the Superior. Then she and I were alone again. We had experienced a genuine *meeting,* so rare and precious in life. She called me her "old-young Mother-Daughter," and I called her my "young-old Granny-Sister," as we still do when we write to one another.

But more than all this was her great gift to me of direction and counsel, a gift that was the turning-point of my journey. She completed the meaning of the message I had received years earlier from another Mother Superior in a convent parlor on Long Island—the message that had baffled me and taken me on this long quest.

"God has something in store for you," she began, speaking out of her own intuition. "You don't have to be a Carmelite, for to join a Carmelite monastery or to found one would limit you, and limit God's possibilities for you. Instead, you must *be Carmel—embody the spirit of Carmel.* Then, whatever God calls you to be or do, you will be free to follow. You can be faithful and free at the same time. We here are your sisters, and we will keep you with us always in the love of our hearts. We will carry you and your ministry in prayer, while you carry us, and our prayer united with your own, into the world." Truly, this was the liberating word I had waited to hear, the clarifying word I'd been seeking. An integration began inside me that is still going on, a process of refinement through many transformations.

On Mother Cyril's advice, I went on to visit the Carmelite community in Vermont, where I had the same kind of reinforcement in an encounter with Mother Mary of the Blessed Sacrament and the others Sisters there. Mother Mary and I also had a meeting of souls. She confirmed everything that Mother Cyril had said to me. Through these women, who are still my friends and sisters in Christ, I became free to face the possibilities of the future. These women, without knowing it at the time, gave me to the priesthood. Today, they participate in my priestly ministry, as Mother Cyril had promised me so long ago, neither of us imagining at the time the full implications of her words.

More immediately, the Carmelites helped me to see that I could incorporate values of prayer and total commitment into Sister Rosaire's and my vision of an ecumenical religious community. What I had learned at the end of my journey was that it is possible to make wholeness out of one's life experience. I could integrate spiritual values from the various traditions in my own background, making of them something that could be meaningful for others.

When I returned to Oregon, I went to my bishop, ready to ask for his endorsement of the Ecumenical Oblates. I obtained his formal endorsement and the ecclesiastical permission to make my own profession in 1968. Though I was still alone, I had a sense of accountability to the future, and I saw my personal vows as a renewal of my baptismal commitment that I made in the context of a community-in-anticipation. I myself had to begin by living out the vision.

I made a profession of commitment, vowing to live my life by Simplicity, Availability, and Purity-as-Wholeness. My bishop had forbidden me to make a vow of celibacy, for which I had occasion to thank him some years later. My vows were my own interpretation of the traditional vows of poverty, obedience, and chastity. For me, chastity and purity are connected to integrity and wholeness. To be a pure human being means to be wholly human, with nothing added to or subtracted from one's humanity. Some achieve sexual integrity through direct sexual activity, and some achieve it through the creative conversion of sexual energy into their life's work, as artists loving their art into being, as scholars or scientists creating new ways of perceiving the world through words and concepts, as celibate philosophers or God-centered people who learn joyfully to express relational love for their co-creatures in unique ways. But I believe now that the choice of celibacy as a means to wholeness is very rarely justified, and needs to be determined by the individual's temperament and whole psychological and physical make-up lest it be a hindrance rather than an enhancement to wholeness. As for poverty and obedience, in our culture poverty is an evil thing associated with rats and hunger, not the straightforward *simplicity* of Christ; and too often obedience translates into blind conformism, irresponsibility—acting only as an agent of someone else's will, never as oneself—an understanding contrary to the responsible openness to Christ in others that I have tried to describe as *availability*.

Becoming an Ecumenical Oblate meant that I had to revise my plans for the external conditions of my life as well as the internal ones. I couldn't rely on a traditional religious order to support me for the rest of my life. I would have to be a responsible tax-paying citizen like most everyone else, which meant that I'd have to have a means of livelihood. For me, this meant at long last going to a university to become credentialed for a profession. Now not only was I prepared to go to college, to the great joy of my father who had been grieving over my refusal of formal intellectual development, but I intended to go for broke by earning a Ph.D. At the same time, I was undergoing another change in self-awareness. I began to own something that I'd disclaimed and suppressed because I didn't see how it was possible: a calling to ordained ministry.

Diaconate

I had finally heard about women in the diaconate, probably the Episcopal Church's best kept secret. The new knowledge that women could be ordained as pastoral ministers enabled me to examine the possibility of ordination for myself. Now that I knew it was possible, I didn't have to hide from myself the fact that I had long felt drawn to ordination. In fact, I felt drawn toward priesthood, but that ministry was still very much in the realm of the impossible. So for the time being I went to speak to my bishop about becoming an ordained deacon. My bishop encouraged me and seemed genuinely supportive of my ecumenical ministry, which would be deepened by the sacramental authority of ordination.

In the fall of 1968, I applied to Northwestern University and to Seabury-Western Theological Seminary on the edge of Northwestern's campus. My plan was to work toward a bachelor's degree at Northwestern and a master's degree at Seabury-Western simultaneously, then later go on for the doctor of philosophy degree. Both institutions accepted me for the following academic year. I was to begin during the summer session at Northwestern, and the fall quarter at the seminary.

I knew that during the five years I'd given myself to gain

the academic credentials I wanted it would be impossible for me to receive others into the Ecumenical Oblates. To prepare myself for that long hiatus, I spent five months in a small ecumenical community on the campus of the University of Portland before I left Oregon.

My ties with the University of Portland were through the Portland Poetry Center, which I had set up in a donated room in one of the buildings on campus there, overlooking the Willamette River. I spent a lot of time on the campus with poetry readings and meetings, and I became acquainted with some of the Roman Catholic Holy Cross Fathers who owned and taught at the University, and with one Benedictine who was very interested in ecumenism. He was a Chinese priest, and he soon invited me to join him and five others who were living on campus in Fischer Hall, an old World War II provisional building owned by the University.

In September I moved into the fruit cellar in the basement. Roman Catholics lived on the main floor, Chinese students practiced Buddhism on the third floor under the roof, and the Episcopalian holed up in the basement—far from sky, near to ground. My tiny room was off the makeshift kitchen and laundry room. It was big enough for a cot, small rug, a large cross made of cherry tree branches on one wall, and my carved wood statue of Our Lady of Mt. Carmel on the other wall. In December I was awakened every morning by a bird who would kick snow off a bush by my window into a chink in the glass over my head.

I was content in my modest *poustinia* those months at Fischer Hall. The Chinese students were given to preparing exotic oriental meals at odd hours of the night. Fine aromas would waft into my room, and I would find a way of inviting myself out into the kitchen to visit with them over some enticing delicacy at three or four in the morning. In October all of us participated in Chinese Moon Festival, a ritual meal supposed to be eaten on roof tops under the full moon to call

78

down blessings for the harvest. Those of us in the house who were Christians broke bread together daily in a makeshift chapel on the second floor. It was a place of intercultural cooperation as well as ecumenism. Everyone who lived there seemed to be mutually enriched by the others.

In February I left Fischer Hall for Evanston and a fresh start in the Midwest, making a physical transplant that has been traumatic and never quite successful.

I travelled through the transition by train, allowing myself time to make the necessary psychological shift from Pacific Northwest to the central states. In Montana a Wild West Wagon was hitched to the train to serve as the dining car. By the time we got to North Dakota, my soul felt as desolate as the endless white wasteland of the central prairies outside. Then Minnesota and the western hemisphere's answer to Siberia: snow, snow, snow—bitter cold and then . . . the endless flatland of the Midwest. Where were the mountains? I had not been weaned away from the three white volcanoes in whose motherly, majestic, and unpredictable shadow I had been raised. This uprooting made me painfully aware of how much the land itself meant to me in the place where I was born, and of how deeply it had affected my personality.

My first impressions of Chicago were not flattering. The native Americans called it "Place of the Big Stink," and always avoided travelling near it because of its bad location over sulfur beds. White pioneers came and built a city there, and industry has intruded its own odors that now overpower any vestige of natural nastiness in the air. Chicago still suffers from a noxious atmosphere—one of political and economic suffocation. I had a taste of it during my first week in the area.

As part of my preparation for ordained ministry I went through a month-long program at the Urban Training Center for Christian Mission in the winter of 1969. As soon as I had unpacked at the National Center for the Diaconate in Evanston, where I lived for nearly three years, I headed back into Chicago for exposure to the inner city.

The Urban Training Center's philosophy was praxis: the interplay of reflection and direct experience. Most of the forty students for that session were southern black Protestant pastors. Three of us were women. Our first praxis came from the experience of "The Plunge." We were each given $6 on the first day of the program, then sent out to survive on the streets of Chicago for the next three nights and days. We wore old clothes and took nothing with us except for the $6. Some of the students were robbed the first afternoon. One of the young men was molested by a gang. We women broke the rules by sticking together. We were too terrified to do it any other way, and we wondered how any woman alone makes it in the city. That was the point of the experience—to make us wonder. We spent our first night in Union Station, where no one talked to us except an Amish family traveling home to Pennsylvania after a funeral in Kansas. The next night at the Clark Theater we saw old women with shopping bags full of pillows and curlers who seemed to take regular lodging in the balcony. We noticed that the proprietors' way of discouraging this was to increase the volume of the movies through the night. By morning we had seen—and heard more and more loudly—*King Kong* and *The Hunchback of Notre Dame* three times. We left at dawn, dazed and grateful that it was Ash Wednesday and we could go to church, warming ourselves through three or four services. A Dominican Sister who was with us noticed some women from her own community in their big new station wagon that nearly hit us going around the corner of State Street and Monroe. I met a Franciscan priest who literally refused to give me the time of day. It was frightening to take off our middle class clothes and face ourselves mirrored in other people. Without the external signs of middle class protection, we briefly became

80

the rejected ones, seeing ourselves in the priest and the polite people who looked the other way as we passed. This was a privileged view from the other side, and we had it for just a moment, just long enough to gain respect for it.

We tasted only the smallest portion of alienation and desperation that characterize inner-city life. We witnessed racism on the streets and in public places, and later we saw it where people lived, in the high rise projects on the north side, in the ghettoes on the south and west side. We learned to look and listen as welfare mothers and unemployed workers taught us about political, economic, and ethnic oppression from their own experience of it. Later we marched with some of them in Jesse Jackson's Hunger Caravan to the state capital at Springfield. The most difficult thing we learned was that white guilt had no place in black self-actualization. We whites had to go back into our middle class communities and confront racism within the social class structures. We had no business staying around the black communities playing savior or sacrificial offering. This was an important time for me. It was my first exposure to urban poverty and racial oppression, and it opened my eyes to the place of politics in Christian social witness. More importantly, it started me thinking about the nature of human oppression, preparing me for a personal encounter with sexism that was not far off.

The parallels between racism and sexism have been drawn countless times, appropriately and inappropriately, and this is not the place to recreate the sketch. But it is the place for me to tell you how the seeds of Christian feminism were planted in my soul by my Christian urban education in the politics of racism.

The Civil Rights Movement evolved into the Black Liberation Movement and the Peace Movement, both of which confronted the quality of life for people of color in particular—black Americans and yellow Vietnamese—at the time of my experience in Chicago. Like many other women, I did not perceive the depth of teaching in the human rights lessons of these movements, even though I was involved in them, for I had not yet been directly, overtly, and personally diminished by sexism. The unconscious diminution I had been subject to all my female life was a reality too deep inside me to see, and I had not yet suffered enough to be able to face it.

Through my protected life I had carried on under the illusion that freedom was an individual possession instead of a corporate right. I enjoyed a false sense of security in what I believed to be my independent status, a private luxury of luck and love that enabled me to function as I chose within the limits of my personal life, a life then cut off from political awareness of the rest of the human community. I had only heard of the Women's Liberation Movement by specious, often malicious, rumor. I knew only what had been extracted by the media. Like most people, I had an accumulation of assumptions which added up to an absurd distortion of the philosophy and politics of the Women's Movement.

I still cringe when I remember the sort of stupid things I thought and said as a patriarchal woman, a "queen bee" who had made it in a man's world and had no need to think of the plight of her sisters, which was in reality her own plight as well. "Equality hell. I wouldn't give up my superior position for anything." I can understand reactionary women today, since I myself once thought such things. The most humbling thing I've ever experienced is that I once said, "If there are ever women priests in the Episcopal Church, I'm going to Rome." And here I am, my own best joke, myself a woman priest in the Episcopal Church, a challenge to my own bigotry! People can change.

I think my problem was that I confused my own ideal with reality. I knew that we had all been freed in Christ, women and men alike, so why speak of liberation when we were already free? What I didn't realize was that we had all been *offered* freedom, but we hadn't yet *taken* it. In fact, we were still trying to keep one another from taking it. I began to see this in my encounter with the oppression of the poor and of people of color through my experiences at the Urban Training Center. Reflection on oppression ultimately led me to deal with my own oppression as a woman in a society that devalues womanhood.

I began to question the inconsistencies between the church's teaching and practice with regard to women. I perceived that the Church that taught me to believe in my human dignity had itself denied me that dignity.

Just as I was beginning to explore this insight my time at the Urban Training Center was over, and I went back to Evanston where I was to undergo my first real shock of unbridled sexism, directed against me through my own Church.

The Rev. Frances Zielinski, director of the Center where I lived, told me that the dean of the seminary wanted to see me to discuss my academic schedule for the following year. I arranged for an interview and she and I went to meet with him one nippy April morning.

When we walked into the dean's office, we were greeted with indignation gradually blooming into ripened rage. It was the best example of bad timing I have ever experienced. It seemed that that very morning an ordained woman who had previously won the dean's disfavor was pictured on the front page of the *Chicago Tribune*. She was shown officiating at the wedding of a counter-culture couple in Berkeley.

The dean had the clipped photograph and article in hand, and he proceeded to pace back and forth in front of us, punctuating his monologue with the clenching and flexing of his fist around the paper in the air. He was beside himself with anger that a woman had received this kind of publicity, which he called "demeaning" to the Church. When our time was nearly up, he turned to address us, acknowledging our presence for the first time. He informed us that he had no intention of allowing any more women into the seminary at that point, that he hoped the present women students would go back where they belonged in the chapel (which meant to the guest gallery in the rear, where they had been formerly required to sit rather than in the choir with the other students), and that he didn't think any woman had "brains enough" to earn two degrees at once. He then rather sneeringly suggested that I come back in four years, when he might reconsider me.

Frances and I left without a word. Speech had been shocked out of us.

Never in my life before or since that morning have I seen anyone in authority behave like that. It was the most purely irrational reaction I have ever witnessed.

Frances and I walked back to the Center together, trying to sort out what had happened. We were both quite shaken, and considered it fitting and medicinal to settle ourselves over a morning glass of sherry. My instinct for survival came into play immediately; I began to consider my alternatives. Certainly I had been confronted by an immovable object, whose force had direct consequences for my future. My personal and professional goals were at stake because of one man's anger at another woman. (How many times in history has this happened, I wonder?) Frances reminded me that Episcopal canon law doesn't require candidates for ordination to attend seminary. Seminary is just the most efficient way of preparing for the intensive canonical exams that canon law does require. There is always the option, in special and extreme circumstances, of private study. My circumstances were extreme. I resolved to take this option, with the consent of my bishop, which I obtained after reporting the morning's incident to him.

Through the following sixteen months I achieved the equivalent of five years of education, taking double course loads at Northwestern to complete two years' work in one, while moonlighting in theology with a lot of help from my friends. The women clergy with whom I lived were tremendously helpful and supportive, not letting me give in to fatigue or discouragement when I was tempted to do so. And I had friends on the seminary faculty, persons who were aware of my situation and offered me the use of their syllabuses, and hours of generously given consultation. I may have had legal recourse—since I had been accepted in writing by the admissions committee, which the dean then countermanded—but nearly everyone in the seminary community was intimidated by this unpredictable man, and the usual recourse was not considered. The assistant dean tried to appeal to him with no success, but he himself offered me personal support by inviting me to audit his own courses in moral and aesthetic theology. I had full access to the seminary library as a Northwestern student. I really had more backing and encouragement than most of the seminarians did, since everyone champions an underdog. As it turned out, I was ready to take the ordination exams in half the time without being limited to a conventional seminary curriculum.

In September of 1970, I went home to take my canonicals in the diocese of Oregon. Although my diocese was a conservative one, and the chairman of the Examining Chaplains Committee was openly against women in holy orders (though he could "live with" female deacons so long as we weren't priests), I had a certain advantage. I was the first woman to be ordained in the diocese of Oregon, and the examining chaplains had no previous experience that might incline them to treat me differently because of my sex, so I was examined in the same way as men in the diocese. This meant that later on I could not be accused of being given special treatment or being allowed to pass under inferior standards of examination. For three days I wrote examinations in systematic theology, Church history, pastoral ministry, moral theology and Christian ethics, liturgics and

85

homiletics, prayer book history and religious education. After a three-hour oral exam on the fourth day, the chief examiner said to me, "You have survived the ordeal by fire. Welcome to the tribe." Suddenly the months of eye strain all seemed worthwhile. I had learned a lot more through the whole process than the content of subject matter in which I had been examined. I had learned (and strange that it took me so long) that sexism does exist, even where we least expect it. And I had learned about my own capabilities and resources for survival. I also learned that it takes personal experience to really make a woman aware that she is oppressed by society, and that my own lifelong response to unconscious feelings of being "not okay" as a female was to prove myself by over-achievement. How well I now recognize these traits in other women, because of my own experience.

The second major trauma I experienced with regard to sexism in the Church had to do with the date of my ordination. I had fulfilled the canonical time requirement for postulants and candidates for Holy Orders, and I had successfully completed the physical, psychological, and academic exams. I had been interviewed by the Standing Committee (the bishop's advisory counsel in each diocese). I was ready to be ordained. But just at that time in 1970, the General Convention meeting in Houston changed the canon law on women in the diaconate, eliminating discriminatory language ("deaconess") and bringing into conformity all standards and regulations for women and men deacons and candidates for ordination.

The chancellor, or legal advisor, of the diocese of Oregon urged my bishop to require me to undergo the entire time period of canonical preparation over again, "so that there would be no confusion as to which canon" I would be ordained under. Even though my bishop checked with other bishops who had female candidates in the same position and found that none of them was making the same demand of other women, he ordered me to follow the chancellor's interpretation of the situation.

I was puzzled by the reasons given for the delay. Male candidates in the past had not been asked to go through candidacy again when the canon on candidates had been changed during their term of candidacy. The chancellor's interpretation and the bishop's acceptance of it seemed to me not only peculiar, but unreasonable and unfair. Yet I had no say in the matter and my protest was taken for insolence, as if I were being a naughty child. I submitted, but I did not submit well. The cordial relationship I had with my bishop began to be strained. I began to ponder the question: How long, O God, how long must a woman wait twice as long and be twice as good for half as much?

Once again, life called upon me to wait, and wait I did. However, I had no time to become bitter, since life was offering me other things that required my best response.

Since Sister Rosaire's death four years earlier, I had lived with the impossible challenge of trying to be a community of one. Though I was clearly alone, I continued to strive for fidelity to a vision that had been born out of my relationship with another Christian woman. The discipline of my life formed around my faithful anticipation of a future community, of sisters and brothers in Christ whom I had not yet found, or who had not yet joined me. I sustained myself with assurances of faith in the future, and I came to see myself in the community with the whole communion of saints, past, present, and to come. Perhaps the most accurate description of those years is that I lived in anticipation of a community as a kind of female monk.

The word "monk" through history has come to mean a male who makes religious vows. But monk really means "one who is alone," coming from the Greek root, *mono*. "Nun," on the other hand, derives in all probability from a Low Latin epithet meaning "old woman." I wasn't an old woman, but I was alone.

Then, in early winfer of 1970, I met a person who called me out of my aloneness and changed my life. Phil Campbell (now Bozarth-Campbell) came to the seminary that fall. He was bright, sensitive, and gifted, a fine musician and a loving person. We shared a mutual excitement for life and for music and the ministry, and soon we discovered that our gifts complemented each other. One day he told me that he wanted to become an Ecumenical Oblate. I was astounded.

Phil made his commitment as my brother in Christ, an Ecumenical Oblate, that spring. We also discovered that we had more to share than our religious vocations.

Marriage

On September 12, 1971, four days after my ordination to the diaconate in the cathedral of the Diocese of Oregon, the man who had become my brother in Christ as an Ecumenical Oblate became my spouse as well. We were married in the garden of Mt. Resurrection Monastery. My father officiated, Brother Andrew and Brother Barnabas served, my mother and Phil's parents were our ring-and wreath-bearers (from a Russian wedding custom), and my goddaughter Veronica carried my train. Two of our close friends sang "Here Comes the Sun," "Amazing Grace," "Follow Me," and "The Lord of the Dance." We composed our own vows. We walked out into the open together, wearing royal blue velvet and white satin Russian style wedding clothes made by my mother, carrying icon- and flower-decked candles into the sunlight. All three snow-clad mountains came out for the occasion—Mt. Hood, Mt. Adams, and Mt. St. Helen's, the sleeping volcanoes under whose influence I had grown up.

During the years of our life together, there have been three occasions for our ministries to illuminate our marriage in a healing way. We have experienced our marriage as a dance in which first one and then the other of us will take the lead according to the needs of both of us in any given moment. So we frequently are aware of the doctrine of exchange at work in our relationship. Within the first year of our marriage, Phil and I became brother and sister in the difficult and sorrowful task of helping my mother during her struggle with cancer. Phil became a son to her as the two of us helped her face her own death. Later, Phil stood close beside me during the Service for the Dead in tiny St. Nicholas Church where I had been baptized, and when we took my mother's body to Canada to be buried by her own mother's grave, Phil spilled earth over her flesh as I officiated at the graveside service. When I had the privilege of burying my mother, the metaphor from the Gospel came alive to me: "Unless a grain of wheat falls into the ground and dies it abides alone; but if it dies it brings forth much fruit." The seed of my mother's body I was planting in the earth was as unlike her new resurrection body as a small shrivelled pine seed is unlike the glorious evergreen tree it will become, yet each is one and the same. Phil's presence with me during this great grieving time was in itself healing, for as I wept for the loss of my mother, Phil became a mother to me in his tenderness and strong compassion; a mother not because of these qualities, but because I needed him to be a *mother* to me.

Three years later, my grandmother died while Phil and I were driving to Oregon from Minnesota for our summer visit. I called my father when we were stopped in a town in Montana to see how grandma was, for I knew that her condition was failing after seven years of constant mental and physical pain following the amputation of both her legs. My father told me that his mother had died that evening. She was free at last. I had said goodby to grandma years before, when we all thought she was dying. No one expected her tremendous stamina to keep her going for such a long time. It was from this great woman that both my father and I received our love and reverence for language, for learning, and for all that is lovely in life. I was deeply moved when papa asked me to be with him and his sister during grandma's funeral, and then told me he counted on Phil to officiate for our family.

90

Phil had never known grandma when she had been herself, but he had inklings of her through my stories and memories, and he could sense the gifted woman inside the fading exterior in those times when he had seen grandma in the nursing home before and since our wedding. He said that he was honored to be able to perform this service for her and for us, and his sensitivity to grandma was beautiful to witness. His words were few and simple, in her own style. Those of us who knew the saga of her life were reminded of her difficult car trip from Missouri to Washington State during the dust bowl years as Phil quoted the preacher from *The Grapes of Wrath*. Grandma, like the old man in the book, just lived her life as best she could and just died right out of it, the same as we will. It's for us now to go on living as best we can, because grandma's got her job cut out for her now and so do we, and it's up to all of us to get on with it.

The summer after my grandma died, Phil's paternal grandmother followed. I had met her one afternoon in Philadelphia the year before, when Phil's mother and I had driven there for my ordination to the priesthood. She was a genteel and gracious woman, a former schoolteacher like my own grandmother. I had a sense of her from our meeting, so when her daughter and son asked me to officiate at her funeral, I was grateful for the opportunity to serve Phil's grandmother and family as he had mine. I did not quote from Steinbeck, but from the film *Rachel, Rachel,* a brief scene in which the title character is coming to after surgery in a recovery room. A nurse says to her, "You're all right. You're out of danger." In her half-awake state, Rachel answers, "That's impossible. I'm not dead yet." Phil's grandmother was finally out of danger, but the rest of us had to go on living.

If our marriage has had its moments of serene sharing as on these sacred occasions of observing the transition into eternity of my mother and both our grandmothers, it began in less than serene circumstances.

When I was ordained, Phil had two years of seminary

still to complete. I was faced with the academic labors of two more degrees myself. We set up housekeeping together in the married students' dorm on the seminary campus. Phil was a middler (second year student) in the seminary whose dean had two years earlier told me to come back in four years. Meantime, I had been judged qualified for ordination, had earned one degree, and had been ordained.

During the next two years I must have been a thorn in the side to the dean, who now had to see me on a daily basis since we shared living space on the same grounds. Occasionally friends of mine who were priests on the seminary faculty would ask me to assist them liturgically at chapel services. These must have been the most difficult times for the dean. When the faculty members came up to the altar for communion, the associate dean who had been my great supporter in years past would go out of his way to cross over to my side of the altar rail in order to take communion from me, while the dean would go as much out of his way to cross over to the other side to avoid me.

During the first year of our marriage Phil and I became committed to defining our relationship on our own terms as we created it. This meant a continuous effort to reject stereotypes. We put up a conscious resistance to external expectations from outside our relationship—assumptions that we perceived in our relatives, friends, colleagues, in our communities, and within society itself.

If the Episcopal Church had opened my eyes to sexism, society's stereotype of marriage became the college text for the subject. My first shock was that people wanted to take my name away from me—my name, the primary symbol of my identity as a person. A married woman in our culture is stripped of her identity layer by layer, symbolically and actually. The old phrase "man and wife" tells the story: in marriage, the man remains a man, but the woman becomes a wife. When I was a child I had to develop a strong sense of self in order to avoid being identified with either of my parents. But as a married woman, for the first time in my life I realized that society expected me to have *no* identity (except in relationship to the man I married). This was an impossible concept for Phil and me, since our relationship has always been built on the mutual sharing of our *selves* in true interdependence. My conversion to the Women's Liberation Movement was made complete that year. Phil and I began to explore Women's and Men's Liberation as the philosophical and political movements toward the freedom promised us by Christ.

Our shared commitment to the Liberation Movement in Church and society grew as we ourselves became more aware of a pervasive, oppressive denial of the freedom of the children of God in our own Church.

Even before our marriage, Phil and I began to share a dream. The dream was that we would be ordained to the priesthood together. Since the General Convention openly raised the issue of women in the priesthood in 1970, I had become able to admit to myself that I had a vocation to the priesthood. It's a vocation I've had all my life, but one I learned to hide from myself because it seemed impossible to fulfill. When a person feels called to be something society says she can't be, she suppresses the inclination rather than live with the pain of its impossibility. I had done that, burying the truth in my bones, moving through that part of my own life like a sleepwalker. But the calling would not go away. Though I tried to leave it, it never left me.

My specific calling to the priesthood rose in my consciousness as a strong inclination toward sacramental life. I experienced this vocation in the way I think most people experience theirs: as the clear direction in which my life was naturally moving, the obvious way in which all the elements of my personality and experience combined. Early on, my bishop had also perceived this calling to priesthood within me, privately encouraging me but publicly working against the ordination of women to the priesthood. Phil also perceived my calling to the priesthood, and he supported it unconditionally, as did my close friends and the other women I came to know who shared the same calling. After the close vote in Houston in 1970, we were naively optimistic about the next vote in Louisville in 1973. By then, Phil would be a deacon, and I would have been a deacon for over two years. (The usual time between ordinations to the diaconate and priesthood for those who seek both offices is six to nine months.)

In spring of 1973, I had completed my year as associate Episcopal chaplain at Northwestern University, and all my doctoral work was done except for the dissertation. Phil graduated from seminary and we moved to Minneapolis, where he had a year's commitment to go through an intern program in his own diocese. We were sure that the October Convention would say yes to women priests, and we could be ordained together the following spring, either in Minnesota or Oregon.

Then, October came, and the General Convention said no. An archaic voting procedure had frustrated the will of the majority for the second time. (Both in Houston and Louisville there were more yes than no votes in the House of Deputies, but there were sufficient divided delegations to defeat the issue.) We had failed to take into account the structural and procedural problems in the House of Deputies. Our dream died; for us it was the beginning of sorrows.

After four generations of women in the Episcopal Church had died waiting for the opening of the priesthood to women, one more generation had been told to wait indefinitely by the vote in Louisville. The vocational bond among women called to priesthood in the Episcopal Church had become a bond of suffering and forbearance as well. Those who observed us from the outside may have had little understanding of our anguish, of the total denial that we felt from our Church. Those who accused us of stridency failed to perceive cries of pain in our voices.

In many cases, our bishops could no longer minister to us, for the suffering we experienced because of the Church's sexism seemed only to bring confusion to some of the great men of God in our midst. Perhaps they felt responsible in their own minds and did not like to be reminded of their part in our pain. Rather than respond to us as pastors, many bishops became personally defensive and aloof, blindly reprimanding us for having the presumption to be in pain in the first place. When our pastors could no longer find access to pastoral grace for us, we turned to one another and discovered the sources of healing among ourselves.

My initial response to the October Convention was numbness. Nature protects us from intolerable pain by causing the organism to go unconscious. As the numbness began to wear off after a month, the nerves of my soul began to stand on end. I began to understand that I was unacceptable as a woman by the very Church that had taught me to celebrate my womanhood. The reality of rejection and alienation colored every waking moment and filled my dreams with bleeding ghosts. Eventually, anger subsided into heartache and deep loneliness. I had no thought of leaving the Church; I felt that it had already left me. The denial of my calling to the priesthood was the denial of me as a child of God. Yet it wasn't Christian people who had denied me, it was a bureaucratic voting procedure.

Meanwhile, Phil's bishop was making plans for his ordination to the priesthood early the next spring—the event that was to have been doubled. Phil needed the affirmation of ordination as much as I did. I couldn't ask him to suppress his own vocation until the Church could accommodate mine. Yet, emotionally, the thought of his being ordained a priest without me was more than I could bear. I tried desperately not to make him feel guilty about a situation that held us both in a vise, but confusion and grief muddied my intentions. Our marriage underwent a dance of death, and it was months into the future before it could begin to be transformed into a dance of rebirth.

That February, we were to visit my father in his mobile home in Palm Springs, California. The night before we left Minnesota, something snapped for Phil in our relationship. He had borne my burden for four months, and he was tired. He was exhausted. There was nothing left for him to give me in the way of comfort and support. He had completely closed off his own needs in order to minister to me, and now his needs were crying out for recognition and attention. The outward signs of this were in Phil's open hostility toward me. Suddenly, for the first time in our relationship, he wanted absolutely nothing to do with me—and yet, he wanted me there beside him. He didn't want to look at me or listen to me, but he wanted to be able to squeeze my arm, even a little more tightly than I could bear. We then began to learn that wrestling can be an aggressive form of passionate embrace.

Our first night in Palm Springs, Phil told me all his negative feelings toward me. I was devastated, numb, in despair. I cried and cried and tried to get near him, to undo what had come between us, but he wanted nothing to do with me. We slept in beds on opposite sides of the room, literally in opposite corners, as they happened to be arranged that way. I cried myself to sleep, and so did Phil. In the middle of the night, I heard him call my name. "What?" I asked. Still half-sleeping, he repeated, "Sweet Alla . . . " "What is it, Phil?"

"Nothing," he said. "I just wanted to say your name."

Then I began to weep out of relief, for I knew that there was some hope for us, that his love for me hadn't been killed, but was temporarily buried under his own pain. The next morning we made an appointment with a psychiatrist in Palm

Springs. As we explained our situation and our feelings to him, he sat on his desk chewing red licorice, listening intently, but with no sign of emotion. When we'd finished, he gave us each a quizzical look, put away his candy, pulled up a chair in front of us, and leaning over with an air of matter-of-fact confidentiality, he said, "I think you should go to New Zealand." It was perfect. Phil and I looked at each other. We both thought he was cracked. "What?" I asked.

"Well," he went on with a shrug that said how logical everything was to him, "it's obvious that your Church has messed things up for you, and you can't do anything about it. So go away for a year and forget it, and be sheep farmers in New Zealand, or go anywhere else you like. But get back down to earth, get back together, and forget all this Church business until it blows over." I thought it was excellent advice. Phil didn't buy it. "Why not?" the shrink asked him. "Do you need your wings that much? I had an air force buddy who had to get his wings before he could do anything with himself. Maybe you're like him and you need your wings?" Phil said he did. "Okay. That's all right. What will that do to you," he asked me, "him getting his wings?"

"I guess if he really needs them, even though I feel I need them too, I should be glad one of us is getting them."

"*Should* be—but what are you really? Glad or mad?"

"Mad. And sad. But I want to be glad."

"Let yourself be mad and sad. That's reasonable. Maybe you can work on it so you don't take it out on Phil?"

"Yes. I don't want to take it out on him."

"Good. I think you're both pretty sane people and can work this out together."

We went back to Minneapolis at the end of ten days in the desert, and Phil began working regularly with a psychotherapist, an older clergyman who was very perceptive. We continued to struggle through the winter into spring. The crisis came one night when life drew us down so low we

97

found ourselves sobbing in each other's arms on our kitchen floor. From then on there was no place for us to go but up.

On March 25, 1974, the Feast of the Annunciation, we celebrated Phil's ordination and my non-ordination to the priesthood. In order to accurately respond to the event, I stood in the doorway in the rear of the church throughout the service, for the Church had effectively shut me out. At the moment in our lives when Phil and I should have been side by side in our ministries, the Episcopal Church had come between us, just as the congregation was physically between us. Everyone present had been given a copy of this statement:

> To Our Sisters and Brothers in Christ:
>
> We are all met here together tonight to celebrate and to share in the Sacrament of Ordination to the Sacred Order of Priests. This Sacrament represents not simply the fulfillment of many years of preparation, academic and otherwise; much more importantly, it represents the fulfillment of a *calling* which demands the commitment of one's whole being. The process of hearing, questioning, doubting, understanding, affirming, and finally answering God's call is one of the most exciting and significant processes of any person's life.
>
> Through these processes, both of us have individually affirmed God's call to us for the Sacred Priesthood. And tonight, the affirmation of only one of us is recognized in this public Sacrament. Because of the technical ruling of the General Convention, the other's affirmation of the priesthood is denied.
>
> This service tonight is, in many ways, a tremendously happy and fulfilling event. Yet at the same time, we feel a great sense of tragedy, waste, and injustice that we cannot both be publicly af-

firmed in our vocations to the priesthood. In all our life together, we have stood side by side in response to God's calling, and it is a painful thing that we cannot do this tonight.

The Church has always represented the wholeness of God to our broken world. Today, the Church itself must be made whole, so that affirmations of *all* Christian vocations may be recognized for all Christian persons, both women and men. It is to this concept of wholeness that we commit ourselves. We call upon and urge all of you to commit yourselves to this wholeness, and to help bring it about, that the Church may indeed be *all* things to *all* people.

Tonight, one of us stands at the front of the church, and one at the back. We stand together, though at opposite ends of the church. We ask you to join us, to be with us, and to pray for us.

In Christ,
        The Rev. Brother Philip, E.O.
        The Rev. Sister Alla, E.O.

As Phil responded to the bishop's examination of the ordinand during the service, I responded too, my voice leaping the space between us. At the time of laying on of hands, most of the priests present went into the chancel to participate in Phil's ordination. One priest, a deacon, and about twelve lay women moved to the back of the church to be with me. My sister deacon in the diocese, Jeannette Piccard, had been standing beside me from the beginning. As the bishop and priests laid sacramental hands on Phil's head, other hands of healing were laid on mine. As I knelt in the doorway confronting the pain and death in that moment, I confronted life in the death center itself, for I felt the healing power penetrating my being from the hands touching me. Phil expe-

99

rienced the sacrament of ordination that night, and I experienced a sacrament of affirmation. It was the turning point for me, a passage from crisis to the quiet waiting place beyond.

Through the following months, Phil and I continued to heal each other and to grow in grace together. We had no idea of what was to come, but we were being made ready.

Priesthood Frustrated

My story's focus is the central life-changing event of my ordination to the priesthood. From the perspective of this focal point the story begins long before my birth.

My story begins in my meeting with Jesus in the gospels. In hearing the liberating word he spoke to the women he met, revealing to them possibilities for themselves that were not apparent in their cultures, I heard that same freeing word spoken to me: Be all you can be. Through my own encounter with the gospels I heard Christ calling me to lay claim on the dignity that is mine as a human being created in the image of God, female.

My story begins as I look to the examples of the heroic women in the Old Testament and their courageous witness to the integrity and holiness of womanhood as God's gift to us of our being. I am learning from their examples to expand my vision of God, to recognize that God is more inclusive than any human idea of deity has ever been. I am learning from holy women of other cultures, ancient and new.

I am learning from the examples of our foremothers in the New Testament communities, and I look to their ministries and the ministries open and hidden of all our sisters in the communion of saints: Lydia the leader, Dorcas the giver who showed compassion, Priscilla the teacher, Phoebe the deacon,

101

and the others—women who responded fully to Christ the Liberator, women who became ministers and valiant leaders of the people they served.

I look to the ministry of Mary Magdalene to whom the risen Christ first appeared. In the truest sense, she is the "Apostle of Apostles," because she was the first one sent by the risen Christ to proclaim the Good News of salvation.

I look to the woman of Samaria as one to whom Jesus entrusted the revelation of his personhood. She was a pre-resurrection apostle and a prophet, for she was sent to her village to speak to others in behalf of the Anointed One. Likewise, she was an evangelist, perhaps the first evangelist, for she generously shared the Good News with her neighbors, as Jesus had commissioned her.

I look to Mary of Bethany who sat with Jesus as a dedicated disciple, and I look to Martha, her hard-working sister whose drudgery was a source of blessedness for those who met and ate at her table

My story begins with their stories, with the hidden history of the great women of our religious tradition from the beginning to the present. History has too often overlooked these women, relegating them to secondary roles in the unfolding drama of Christianity when in fact they are central figures.

The impact of women in the early Church and through history has often been obscured by biased male historians who portrayed them as passive recipients and re-actors instead of active participants and agents in the creation of our religious tradition.

We know that leadership in the early Church was shared by apostles, deacons, and elders or presbyters. The presbyters were given the title of "Elder One" in recognition of their distinctive gifts of wisdom and leadership. They were those who spoke, judged, and acted with authority. They were the spiritual leaders and guides in their communities. According to this understanding, Lydia was certainly a presbyter in the

102

Church at Philippi, and Paul encourages the community there to *help these women who are your leaders.*

In New Testament communities neither men nor women are priests in the sacerdotal sense of Old Testament times or modern times. The only priest in the New Testament is Jesus the Christ, our great High Priest whose sacrifice is complete for all people in all times, as the theologian in the Letter to the Hebrews so beautifully illustrates.

Today, sacramental ministers or priests are said to participate in the priesthood of Christ, symbolic and representative of the priestly participation of all baptized persons. Only very recently has this begun to be true, for a one-sided and exclusive male priesthood represents a one-sided and exclusive community, and not the integrated community of all who are baptized in Christ.

We do not know much about the ministry of women in post-biblical and medieval times. There is much evidence that their influence and authority in the Church were felt more than is true today, just as the gospels are filled with evidence that Jesus honored and respected women a great deal more than many of his future followers did or do.[1]

The fact remains that the male and female followers of Jesus belonged to a culture that was and is still patriarchal, and the political structure and distribution of power in the communities of faith were determined by the social climate of the times as well as by the guidance of the Holy Spirit. Therefore, when the liberating influence of Christ's presence and power was directly or closely experienced, it had the effect of cultural transcendence in the communities who were its witnesses. As

---

[1] For fuller discussion of the relationship of Jesus to women see *Jesus According to a Woman,* by Rachel Conrad Wahlberg (Paulist Press, 1975); *Women and Jesus,* by Alicia Craig Faxon (United Church Press, 1973); and "Jesus Was a Feminist," by Leonard Swidler, in *Catholic World,* January, 1973.

103

the immediacy of this influence wore off, power struggles, jealousies, and male domination took over once again in the Churches. People submitted to the encroaching habits of former structures rather than to the authority of the Holy Spirit, and prevailing social injustices became adapted to the Church instead of being redeemed by it.

For many centuries women in the Western Church had been deprived of full participation in Christian leadership.[2] This situation changed only a little in the early 1860's when the Church of England reopened the diaconal ministry to women. (In history, the integrity of the diaconate had become lost as it was reduced to a mere stepping-stone to the priesthood, an unfortunate accident of time.) The reinstitution of the diaconate as a distinct ministry with its own integrity coincided with the revival of monastic orders in the Anglican Communion.[3] The Church of England expanded the number of rooms in its mansion by knocking down some historical walls and making

---

[2] For documentation of the hidden history and authority of women in the Church see *The Lady Was a Bishop,* by Joan Morris (Macmillan, 1973).

[3] In the Anglican Communion (of which the Episcopal Church is a member), there are three orders of fully ordained clergy: deacons (in the diaconate), priests (in the priesthood), and bishops (in the episcopate); each order has its own functions. The three orders are the forms of apostolic ministry agreed on by the Catholic Church. Holy orders are not to be confused with religious orders: holy orders are conferred upon *ordained clergy;* religious orders consist of *monastic communities.* They are separate areas of commitment. A person may be in one or the other, neither or both, in the expression of a religious vocation. Continuity is in the fact that both clergy (in the Catholic traditions, deacons, priests, or bishops) and members of monastic or religious communities (monks and nuns, or Sisters and Brothers) are *under vows:* ordination vows (*to be* a deacon, priest, or bishop), or monastic vows (to live as a *professed* religious person, usually under forms of poverty, chastity, and obedience, the traditional vows of religious orders in the Western (non-Eastern Orthodox) Churches. The Anglican and Roman Catholic Churches have traditional religious orders (Franciscans, etc.), as well as ordained ministries.

possible again some options for Christian dedication that were very ancient indeed.

However, some of the new forms had inherent problems for women. Women in religious orders were usually under obedience to a male priest, and women in holy orders were treated ambiguously by the hierarchy. The ordained women were called "deaconesses" in deference to Victorian notions of etiquette and in defiance of the ungendered English language. This linguistic artifice enabled the enforcement of discrimination against women in the diaconate that was to cross the Atlantic Ocean and deter the lives and ministries of English and American women for generations.

In America, the first ordinations of Episcopal women took place in 1845, without legal sanction by canon law and without precedent. The Episcopal General Convention of 1889 acknowledged and approved the existence of the Order of Deaconesses in the Protestant Episcopal Church in the United States of America many years after the fact. (Nearly a century earlier Samuel Seabury had been irregularly consecrated the first American bishop in the Episcopal Church. For over half a decade, until the first General Convention recognized him, Seabury's episcopate was open to question. I find it interesting that in the cases of the first bishop as well as the first female deacons—and priests—in the Episcopal Church, political reality necessitated prophetic action.)

The Book of Common Prayer refers to ordained bishops, priests, and deacons as persons "set apart." For the first fifty years or so of their existence, women in the diaconate were not only set apart, but often set aside as well. When I lived at the National Center for the Diaconate a frequent source of hilarity was the arrival in the mail of a donation to support the ministry of "those women who have been set aside by the Church." All too often it was no joke, but sad reality.

Generations of faithful and dedicated women in the

ministry were ordained by laying on of hands by a bishop as were their male counterparts. But afterward they were not treated in the same manner as the men with whom they shared diaconal ministry. Instead they were looked on as "something different"—nobody seemed to know just what. They were required to wear garb that resembled a nun's habit even though (except for a few women clergy who were also members of religious orders) they were not monastics. Even more significantly, they were the only group of individuals in the Episcopal church who were required *de facto* to be celibate—even though they made no vow of celibacy. And this was true until 1964.

In 1920 the Lambeth Conference of Anglican bishops from all over the world declared "deaconesses" to be fully ordained clergy within holy orders. In 1930, at its next meeting, the Lambeth Conference withdrew its affirmative statement. The confusion surfaced as suppression of the women, for upon ordination the authority of the diaconate was conferred on women as well as men, but only the men were allowed to exercise their authority. If an ordained male was available within a hundred miles, an ordained female was likely never to function liturgically. At least this was so in more densely populated areas. The women were not usually found in city centers. Perhaps because of the celibacy they often went where no man would go. They lived out their hidden ministries bravely, unself-consciously, heroically, in Appalachia, on Indian reservations, in the western mountains and northern wilderness, and later in rural ghettoes and urban slums.

In these remote places it was often the case that the ordained woman would be the only minister in the Christian community. When this was so, she did indeed function as fully as her office allowed. She was the one who married, buried, comforted, worked, and lived among her people as one who serves. When it came time for the most important event of the community, the Holy Eucharist, the true minister of the people would have to call upon a stranger from outside, a male priest.

Imagine a situation in which a man would have to travel to some remote spot by horse or mule for more than a hundred miles. Then imagine a community having to interrupt its life when the priest arrived in order to gather together under the leadership of this weary man who was a stranger to them while their own minister, a woman, had to stand aside from the very heart of the community's worship—because she was not a priest, because she was a woman. This kind of thing was played out through four generations of ordained women, women who were deacons, not priests. I know a woman deacon in her seventies now who used to teach male seminarians how to celebrate the Eucharist, though she herself could never actually do it. Of course, not all deacons want to be or are in any way called to be priests. But there were those who did want to and probably were called who couldn't be priests because they were part of an institution that discriminated against their sex.

Deacons are pastoral ministers; priests are sacramental ministers; bishops are overseers. The actual priestly *function* involves only three acts, sometimes referred to as the ABC's of the priesthood: absolving, blessing, and consecrating the bread and wine at the Eucharist. The priest is primarily one who makes sacrifice—one who makes holy, from the Latin *sacer* + *facere*. In the Old Testament, only the male descendants of Aaron could be priests, could offer sacrifice in the Temple on behalf of the priestly community of Israel, while the male descendents of Levi had a liturgical function similar to that of deacons in the ministry of the Word, and the High Priest was the prototype of our bishops. Women had nothing at all to do with these holy functions because they were thought to be unclean. Since there was no distinction between the physical and moral or spiritual for the Hebrews, physical uncleanness meant spiritual inferiority and moral unworthiness. Women were excluded from the holy mysteries because of male ignorance of female biology.

While we have grown more sophisticated in our modern scientific approach to sexuality, deep psychological fears lie latent within the patriarchal psyche. Women are no longer exlcuded from nearness to the holy on the basis of our uncleanness. No one will say outright that women will contaminate the holy, but some will say that we "contaminate the purity of the faith," which means, I suppose, that we threaten the well-preserved continuity of male domination in a waningly patriarchal ministry.

How is it that in the past, women could be deacons but not priests or bishops? An unconscious factor may be a carry-over from the Levitical proscriptions against menstruating (contaminating) women. My guess is that the taboo against uncleanness covered a more primitive and much stronger fear of the female blood taboo. Earliest men must have thought: "What magic have these female creatures who bleed and do not die, out of whose bodies signs of death and life come forth?" The real fear is one of power, not contamination. But today all of this lies on the level of the cultural unconscious. The conscious factor may be that in the minds of many the diaconate is a ministry of service and caring while the priesthood and episcopacy are ministries of spiritual leadership and authority: it is all right for women to be caring servants, but not authoritative leaders. Also, many hold that the priest represents Christ to the people, and since Jesus was male, no woman can do this. Yet Christ is not physically re-presented in the person of the priest. Theologically speaking that is to confuse the priest with the Holy Communion itself, to take the sacrificer for the Sacrifice.

The priest represents Christ in the same way that every baptized person does, through her or his Christ-centered, loving humanity, and in a spiritual, moral, and figurative way.

If women can't represent Christ to the world, then we can't be Christians, let alone priests. If we can, then our priesthood is as authentic as our baptism.

In the Episcopal Church such problems of definition have affected women in and out of holy orders. The policy-making instrument of the Episcopal Church is its General Convention that meets nationally every three years. Until recently women in orders and lay women were equally excluded from this body. Even if the debate were settled as to whether or not "deaconesses" were clergy, they could not have been represented in General Convention since all deacons are politically disenfranchised in the Episcopal Church. (Deacons may not be delegates to General Convention, may not be on Standing Commissions or, in many dioceses, on diocesan committees, and may not be tried by their peers in ecclesiastical court. Neither laity nor other clergy are categorically restricted as deacons are. This is due, in my view, to a general misunderstanding of the office of deacons, and a gross neglect of the theology of ministry with respect to deacons.)

The two houses of General Convention function similarly to the American Congress. The House of Bishops consists of bishops and operates straightforwardly. The House of Deputies consists of supposedly representative clergy and laity. "Clergy" is still defined as priests, and "laity," until 1970, was defined as lay *men*. Women had neither voice nor vote in the bicameral body that governed our ecclesiastical lives, a situation much worse than taxation without representation, for having no control over our spiritual destinies in the Church is a form of suppression, and is more than taxation. In effect, the Episcopal Church had cut itself off from the source of grace and the Holy Spirit in its female members who had no access to decision-making and due process within its structure.

In 1934, Episcopal women petitioned the General Convention for their right to be seated in the House of Deputies. It took twelve consecutive Conventions for this request to be honored. 1970 was the first year in which lay women could be legally seated as delegates to the General Convention. It was that same year that the General Convention, meeting in Houston, eliminated once and for all the discriminatory canon on "deaconesses," declaring them to be women in the diaconate on a par with male deacons. For the first time, ordained women were clearly and unequivocally acknowledged to be what they were: fully ordained clergy, complete deacons.

It was no coincidence that 1970 was the year of recognition for women in ministry, for women themselves brought about the recognition. The inclusion of lay women in the national decision-making body represented another beginning. One phase of the struggle yielded to another. Ordained and lay women still had to join forces in the larger task of full inclusion and recognition of the humanity and holiness of all women in Church and society, a task that has by no means been accomplished.

The artificial barriers of clericalism were necessarily transcended in the common struggle against ecclesiastical oppression through mutual cooperation between lay women and their ordained sisters. In spite of the fact that clericalism usually favors clergy, women deacons had less political power than lay women, a fact that aided solidarity. We were able to learn from one another through these processes that all forms of Christian ministry are equally valid and valuable to our corporate Christian life. We were also able to learn that we did not want to buy into the power structure as it stood, a structure that tended to separate rather than to unite people. Again, we confronted the problem of definitions, exposing the old, creating the new.

The word "clergy" means *chosen by lot.* The word "laity" means *people.* For years we had been laboring under the growing impression communicated in language, liturgy, and pastoral relationships, that clergy were not people and that laity were not important.

Every bishop, priest, or deacon is also a lay person, part of
110

God's *laos* (people). A deacon is a lay person chosen by God and community to focus on pastoral ministry and to be an icon of the pastoral ministry of the community. A priest is a lay person chosen by God and community to focus on sacramental ministry and to be an icon of the sacramental life of the community. A bishop is a lay person chosen by God and community to focus on authority and to be an icon of the prophetic authority of the community. A lay person is the primary Christian minister, baptized into the ministering community, the community that serves the world in love in the name of Christ. Likewise, ministers called to specific functions within the community as deacons, priests, or bishops, are first and foremost *ministers*—that is, *servants*. We are all ordained—ordered—by Christ to proclaim the Good News with our lives.

The problem in the past was that the ministry of women in the Church was frustrated, because even though Christ had ordained us by calling us to the sacramental ministry of priesthood, or the administering ministry of episcopacy, we were hampered by Church policy from exercising those ministries to the full. We could not serve as we were called to, and in our lives, the Good News became too often muted as our own voices were silenced.

The political issue of women priests and bishops was first voted on during the Episcopal General Convention in 1970 in Houston, and again in Louisville in 1973. It was defeated both times by a narrow margin in the House of Deputies because of the so-called divided vote.

Controversial issues were usually decided upon in the House of Deputies by means of a vote by orders, in which clergy and laity vote separately by delegation. One delegation, consisting of four lay persons or four priests from each diocese, must come up with one "yes" or one "no" vote. A tie within the delegation means that the vote is cast *divided* and in effect becomes *no*.

In 1970 and 1973 a majority of delegations voted "yes"

111

over those that voted "no," but in both cases there were enough divided votes to defeat the issue. Depending on the distribution of delegates it is conceivable that as much as an 89% majority may be needed to carry a resolution; in other words, any issue could be defeated by as little as 12% of all votes cast.

With these procedural obstacles involved, those of us who sought priesthood and those others who desired a whole priesthood for the Church had little hope that the General Convention would ever be the avenue through which our desires could be realized. I have already described to you some of the personal despair I experienced after the Louisville Convention in October of 1973. After the initial numbness, followed by the grief and rage of helplessness, I began to experience the political dimensions of our situation as women called to the priesthood within the Episcopal Church.

Laws aren't created in the abstract, they follow upon reality. Until the reality of women priests existed, the Church had no means to deal with the issue except in the abstract. As long as people were talking about principles, no one had to face facts. "A nice idea, but I wouldn't want my sister to marry one!" may have been the thought of more than one male priest or bishop when the subject came up in years and months past. As Gordon Allport says, "Most people do not become converts in advance: they are converted by the *fait accompli.*"

What the Episcopal Church needed was a *fait accompli.* God was soon to provide.

Priesthood Fulfilled

Since the October Convention, action groups of concerned Episcopalians had been mobilizing around the country. The two-year-old Episcopal Women's Caucus focused on the ordination issue and raised the larger question of sexism in the Church. Priests organized to support their sisters. Some male deacons had publicly declared their refusal to be ordained to the priesthood until the women in their dioceses could be ordained priests. Lay women and men recognized a state of emergency in a Church that continued to allow a voting technicality to keep us from wholeness as Christian women and men, equal heirs of the glory of God. St. Irenaeus had said that the glory of God is humankind fully alive, and the Episcopal Church was still choosing death.

In June, 1974, the dam broke when two Episcopal men—a priest and a lay person—publicly challenged the Episcopal Church's bishops to act for righteousness' sake.

Dr. Charles Willie, who was then vice president of the House of Deputies, a prominent black leader, and a professor of urban studies and education at Harvard, preached a sermon at St. Mark's Episcopal Church in Syracuse, New York, on June 9. He said

> ... If Christianity is preeminently the religion of the humble, then it is time that, in humility, we state that

113

we know not God but yet have faith in God's glorious ways and that we are open to the revelation of
God in whatever form God may be revealed in our
contemporary society. And suppose God's will is
revealed by a woman? How dare we decide that she
should not be a priest. . . . Of course, you know that
the General Convention . . . voted against the ordination of women [to the priesthood and episcopate].
I am uncertain that the will of the Episcopal Church
on the ordination of women and the will of God are
the same.

Moreover, Jesus taught us that unjust laws
should be disobeyed when they conflict with the will
of the Lord. As an officer of General Convention, I
state my humble belief that the Church which for-
bids the ordination of women [to the priesthood and
episcopate] is acting on the basis of an unjust law.
And so it is meet and right that a bishop who believes
that in Christ there is neither Greek nor Jew, male
nor female, ought to ordain any . . . person who is
qualified for Holy Orders. A bishop who, on his own
authority, ordains a woman deacon to the priesthood
will be vilified, and talked about, but probably not
crucified. Such a bishop would be following the path
of the Suffering Servant, which is the path Jesus
followed. It requires both courage and humility to
disobey an unjust law. The Church is in need of such
a bishop today.

Many of us had observed that it wasn't even a matter of
disobeying an unjust law, for a literal interpretation of the law,
using generic understanding of the language, supported the
ordination of women as priests and bishops. The canon law on
deacons used male pronouns and was interpreted to include
women. The canon law on priests, written in parallel construc-

tion and using similar language, was interpreted not to include women. There can be no legal justification for inconsistent interpretation of two laws of parallel construction and language. Inconsistency reveals discrimination. What we needed was a bishop with the courage to interpret the law fairly and inclusively. Such a bishop would be "disobeying" custom, perhaps, but only in obedience to the just and inclusive law of God.

On June 15, the Rev. Edward Harris, then dean of the Philadelphia School of Divinity, preached at a service of ordination to the diaconate in the diocese of Pennsylvania. He emphasized the same challenge: the Church must respond in obedient faith to the call of the Spirit to ordain qualified women to the priesthood and episcopate,

> in order to express and celebrate the fact that in Jesus Christ God has delivered us from all structures of domination and privileged access to power. Only so does the Church realize its true mission to be the chief representative of a liberated humanity and in its ordained ministry to be the revealer of what leadership and authority are like in an authentically human community. Says the Roman Catholic theologian Gregory Baum: "The ordination of women to the priesthood would restore a prophetic quality to the Church's ministry, educating people to discern the injustice in present society and presenting them with an ideal for the participation of women in the life of society." By ordaining women to the priesthood the Church can begin to assume the shape of a community which truly represents redemptive reconciliation with God and with all persons. It can thus begin to re-shape the direction of society and enable a genuine freeing of men and women to be in each other's eyes more nearly what God made us to be.

. . . That is how I see it. And believing and feeling as I do, I have no choice but to call for the ordination of women to the priesthood *now*. . . . I call upon the bishops of our Church to ordain to the priesthood without further delay those women who are presently deacons with proper time in office and who have in fact been called and qualified by God. In doing this I also call myself to support them. And I pray that this may be, as it is intended, a proclamation of the Gospel—that God has acted for us and expects us to respond in ready obedience.

In response to the prophetic challenge of these separate proclamations, a meeting of concerned persons was called in Philadelphia on July 10, 1974. Through the day of prayer, discussion, and decision, plans were made for the July 29 ordinations.

The Rev. Paul Washington offered the use of the Church of the Advocate in behalf of his parish. The three ordaining bishops were present at the meeting, as were six women deacons, all of whom were among the Philadelphia ordinands. From the onset of the meeting, attention was focused on the impasse created by the inaction of diocesan bishops who refused to ordain women to the priesthood *even though no written law prohibited it*. The approval of the General Convention, while supportive, was not necessary to change *interpretation* of the law, which every diocesan bishop had authority to do: we are the Episcopal Church, not the Conventional Church. Each bishop is accountable for interpreting and enforcing the law of the Church in the light of the Gospel, the light of justice and freedom and loving inclusiveness. The group of twenty-one lay and clergy persons finally agreed: "Christian charity requires that the impasse be broken by action." The appropriate action was the immediate ordination of women to the priesthood.

116

On July 11, at five o'clock in the afternoon, my telephone rang. It was the Rev. Katrina Swanson, one of the deacons who had been present at the Philadelphia meeting on the tenth. I was on her list of other ordained women to be notified of the decision and invited to participate in the ordinations.

Katrina's first words to me were, "How would you like to be ordained to the priesthood before the end of the month?" I bodily left the ground, responding, "Yes! Yes! Yes!" Somewhere in midair I realized that this was a call to prophetic action as well as a call to ordination. I came back down and said, "Oh my God. *How?*"

Then Katrina told me the sequence of events that I've just described. She reminded me that if I accepted the call and presented myself at the Church of the Advocate on July 29, I risked being deposed, being punitively deprived of all the functions of my ministry.

My first thoughts were the possible consequences of my action for members of my family: my father in his ministry with the Society of St. Paul, my spouse in his new ministry, my mother-in-law in her capacity as president of the Minnesota Episcopal Church Women. I also fleetingly wondered what would become of the eighty job applications I had made since receiving my Ph.D. a month earlier. My career as a seminary professor would probably have to wait while I served time as a rebel. All of this was too much to grasp all at once. I told Katrina—and myself—that I'd pray and think about it for three days and call her back with my decision.

In my heart, I knew that my first response was the only one possible: *Yes.* But I was terrified. I shook for an hour, precisely because I knew that I could do nothing else. I collected myself with the idea that I would act *as if* my decision were *Yes,* thus giving myself time to get used to it.

For the next few days, I got all of the necessary canonical papers in order and sent them to the Standing Committee. Fortunately, I had transferred to the diocese of Minnesota after the Louisville Convention, because Phil and I had decided to stay here for the next General Convention in Minneapolis in 1976. I now had to inform the bishop of Minnesota of the ordination plans.

He and I were scheduled to officiate together at the wedding of friends in Detroit Lakes, Minnesota. After the wedding I asked to meet with the bishop privately. We went to an air conditioned restaurant on that scorching afternoon, and Phil and I told him about the Philadelphia meeting and the proposed ordinations on July 29. The bishop had bought a newspaper on our way into the restaurant, and it remained folded face down on the table between us for the next hour. I later learned that an announcement of the ordinations appeared in a prominent place in that very edition. By the grace of God, we were able to break the news to him before he read it in a press release.

I asked the bishop of Minnesota to come to Philadelphia himself, and participate in the ordinations. As it stood, the ordaining bishops were not diocesan bishops with jurisdiction, but were either retired or resigned. If just one diocesan bishop had ordained a woman in his jurisdiction, or authorized another bishop to do so in his behalf, the question of legality would have been avoided. Our ordinations were irregular not because canon law prohibited women priests, but because we weren't ordained by our own diocesan bishops, or with the consent of our Standing Committees. (The Minnesota Standing Committee received our papers and then filed them away, on the bishop's advice, because we were women. Almost immediately after the ordinations, other Standing Committees began to process papers of women applying for the priesthood, recognizing that the law could be interpreted to include us. Ironically, my papers were kept on file by my Standing Committee for over two years, while the Philadelphia event seemed to have broken the barrier for others.)

The legal breakthrough with regard to ordination to the priesthood itself did not come in Philadelphia, since our

118

diocesan bishops rejected the opportunity to ordain us themselves. My bishop declined to do so in order to avoid dissension in the House of Bishops. He said that he wished I wouldn't go, and that the ordinations wouldn't happen, because they would create confusion over authority in the Church. I told him that I had to go, and that I hoped he understood that, as I understood his reason for not going. There was sadness but resignation between us as we parted, each saying "God bless you," to the other.

My next task was to inform my family and friends, so they, too, could hear the news from me instead of the newspapers. I hesitated to tell my father, who, since my mother's death two years earlier, had become more, not less protective of his only child. I was amazed and delighted when he responded to my news: "That's wonderful! I only wish I felt well enough to be there myself! Tell Phil to put both hands on your head during the ordination—one hand for me."

When I had been most frightened during the weeks before the Philadelphia ordinations, I found courage in the first chapter of Jeremiah, who was probably second only after Jonah in the line of reluctant prophets in the Old Testament. Jeremiah, truly a prophet and a great person of God, felt just as afraid and inadequate as I did. I was relieved to discover this, as I told you near the beginning of my story.

On the evening before our ordinations in a gathering of family and friends at Bishop DeWitt's home in Ambler, Pennsylvania, we were openly sharing our feelings and thoughts about the ordinations. I told the group about my own lack of bravery, and how I'd found courage from Jeremiah in this beautiful passage, which I then paraphrased:

The word of God was addressed to me, saying:

Before I formed you in the womb I knew you;
before you came to birth I consecrated you;

119

I have appointed you as prophet to the nations.

I said, "Ah, great God, look,
I do not know how to speak: I am only a *woman*.

But God replied, "Do not say 'I am only a *woman*.'
Go now to those to whom I send you and say whatever
    I command you.
Do not be afraid of them, for I am with you to protect
        you—
it is God who speaks!"

Then God put out a hand and touched my mouth
    and said to me,
"There! I am putting my words into your mouth.
Look, today I am setting you over nations and over
    kingdoms,
to tear up and to knock down, to destroy and to
    overthrow,
to build and to plant. . . .

So now brace yourself for action.
Stand up and tell them all I command you. . . .
They will fight against you but shall not overcome you,
for I am with you to deliver you. It is God who speaks."

   Then Katrina Swanson's son William spoke: "We all have
to carry the cross of Jesus. That's why I'm glad my mom will be
ordained a priest tomorrow, and why I hope my grandfather
will ordain her." Bishop Welles, Katrina's father, had been
uncertain of the degree of his participation in the ordinations,
but I believe that his decision to join Bishop DeWitt and
Bishop Corrigan the next morning was not unconnected with
his grandson's testimony.

Until faced with the extraordinary event of our ordinations, many of us hadn't considered the prophetic dimension of the ordination of women to the priesthood. I quote a significant passage on prophecy and the priesthood of women from the "Statement on the Ordination of Women," by the Anglican-Roman Catholic Consultation:

> . . . [The ecumenical] process of mutual consultation . . . must not interfere with the interacting roles of prophecy and authority within either Church. The entire body of the faithful is in Baptism anointed with the Spirit, and this one same Spirit, distributing diverse gifts at will, at times manifests itself to the entire body through the prophetic witness of a few, for the sake of the whole. It is the proper role of authority in the Church to encourage and promote discernment of such witness, thus fostering an authentic development while at the same time maintaining the integrity of a normative Christian life and tradition.

It is humbling to find oneself in a position of prophetic interplay with the authority of the Church. Each of us at times is called to challenge the body of which we are all a part, in this way claiming co-responsibility for the integrity of the whole. We all stand at different degrees of relationship to the whole, and each of us is called to respond from our unique angle of vision.

The miracle of the Philadelphia ordinations was in their symbolic power and value for women and men not only within, but far beyond the boundaries of the Episcopal Church, or of the Christian tradition. The event constituted a symbolic breakthrough for women everywhere in our ability to fully participate in the mainstream of human spiritual life.

About ten days before the ordinations, our ordaining bishops had released this open letter:

> On Monday, July 29, 1974, the Feast of Saints Mary and Martha, God willing, we intend to ordain to the sacred priesthood some several women deacons. We want to make known as clearly and as widely as we can the reflections on Christian obedience which have led us to this action.
>
> We are painfully conscious of the diversity of thinking in our Church on this issue, and have been deeply sobered by that fact. We are acutely aware that this issue involves theological considerations, that it involves biblical considerations, that it involves considerations of Church tradition, and that it raises the vexing question of amicable consensus in our household of faith.
>
> We are convinced that all these factors have been given due consideration by the Church at large, and by us. We note that the House of Bishops is on record as being in favor of the ordination of women [to the priesthood]. We note that a majority of the clergy and laity in the House of Deputies is also on record as being in favor, even though an inequitable rule of procedure in that House has frustrated the will of the majority.
>
> All of the foregoing factors, by themselves, would not necessarily dictate the action we intend. Nor, even, would this intended action necessarily be required by the painful fact that we know pastorally the injustice, the hurt, the offense to women which is occasioned by the present position of our Church on this issue.
>
> However, there is a ruling factor which does require this action on our part. It is our obedience to

the Lordship of Christ, our response to the sovereignty of His Spirit for the Church.

One of the chief marks of the Church is its being the community of the Resurrection. Ours is a risen Lord. He was raised in the power of the Spirit so that we might participate, however inadequately, in His triumph against sin and separation, proclaim the good news of His victory, and occasionally ourselves walk in newness of life. His Spirit is the Lord of the Church. Hearing His command, we can heed no other. We gladly join ourselves with those who in other times and places, as well as here and now, have sought obedience to that same Spirit.

This action is therefore intended as an act of obedience to the Spirit. By the same token it is intended as an act of solidarity with those in whatever institution, in whatever part of the world, of whatever stratum of society, who in their search for freedom, for liberation, for dignity, are moved by that same Spirit to struggle against sin, to proclaim that victory, to attempt to walk in newness of life.

We pray this action may be, as we intend it, a proclamation of the Gospel—that God has acted for us, and expects us, in obedience, to respond with appropriate action.

The Rt. Rev. Daniel Corrigan
The Rt. Rev. Robert DeWitt
The Rt. Rev. Edward Welles, II

On July 20, the eleven women deacons had released an open letter to our friends in the struggle:

TO: The Episcopal Women's Caucus, Priests for the Ministry of the Church, Priests for the Ordina-

123

tion of Women, The Taskforce on Women, Diocesan Committees to Promote and Plan for the Ordination of Women, Women Seminarians, Women Candidates, Women Deacons.

Dear Friends,

God willing, on Monday, July 29th, the Feast of Saints Mary and Martha, three retired or resigned bishops will ordain to the priesthood eleven women deacons from eight dioceses of the Episcopal Church. We know this ordination to be irregular. We believe it to be valid and right. We are anxious to share with you who have supported this ordination of women to the priesthood the reasons we take such action now.

Enclosed is an open letter from the ordaining bishops. We rejoice in their courage and feel privileged to join them in this act of Christian obedience. We are certain that the Church needs women in priesthood to be true to the Gospel understanding of human unity in Christ. Our primary motivation is to begin to free priesthood from the bondage it suffers as long as it is characterized by categorical exclusion of persons on the basis of sex. We do not feel we are "hurting the cause," for the "cause" is not merely to admit a few token women to the "privilege" of priesthood. We must rather re-affirm and recover the universality of Christ's ministry as symbolized in that order [of priests].

We do not take this step hastily or thoughtlessly. We are fully cognizant of the risks to ourselves and others. Yet we must be true to our vocations—God's irresistible will for us now. We can no longer in conscience answer our calling by

124

saying "Eventually—when the Church comes around to accepting us."

We welcome your support; we earnestly request your prayers. Above all, we urge you to continue the best way you know how in the struggle to bring closer to reality the Pauline promise that "there is neither male nor female for we are all one in Christ Jesus."

Your Sisters in Christ,

Merrill Bittner, Alla Bozarth-Campbell, Alison Cheek, Emily Hewitt, Carter Heyward, Suzanne Hiatt, Marie Moorefield, Jeannette Piccard, Betty Schiess, Katrina Swanson, Nancy Wittig.

In the weeks before July 29, many women deacons over the country were informed of the ordination plans and given opportunity, as I was, to decide whether or not to be ordained to the priesthood in this irregular way. First I heard rumors that there were to be six of us, and then eight, and then twelve, as women conveyed their intentions to participate in the ordinations. My mind's appreciation for symbolism and balance gave me pleasure in thinking that there were to be twelve of us—apostles in the New Tradition! So when, a week before the ordinations, Katrina told me that the final number of ordinands was to be eleven, I was a little disappointed. (In fact, there never were to be twelve. The information had been wrong.) I pondered this number for some time, and wrote this poem months later in retrospect:

New Apostles, New Wine

Imcomplete, they call us,
unrecognizable.

125

Because we are eleven
and not the Magic Twelve
of your chosen few?
Because we are female
(nigger-women)
and not important enough
to mention in Matthew,
Mark, Luke or John,
our Hebrew sisters present
at your First Feast?

We are the flesh
of your mother and sister,
we are the life of the world.
We are new wine bursting
old skins.
Not twelve, but Eleven:
Judas is gone
and we wait your Coming,
prophets of your resurrection.

So it happened. On July 29, the Feast of Saints Mary and
Martha, eleven women were ordained to the priesthood in the
Church of the Advocate in the City of Filial Love. The Church
died and began to be reborn. Tradition was not broken but
fulfilled. Transcended in its structure and transformed in its
soul, the Episcopal Church would never be the same again: not
because women were "saving" the Church (for we have only
the same capacity for sanctity and sin as our brothers), but
because at last the fullness of the Gospel had the possibility of
being spoken to and through all of God's people, for the
barrier that kept women from the freedom and dignity of the
children of God was being broken.

That historic day began like any other in Philadelphia. It

was beastly hot and humid when we met in the vesting room of the Church of the Advocate at ten in the morning. The eleven of us vested in appropriate garb for the occasion—white albs and red stoles worn over one shoulder in diaconal style. We were waiting to join our priest and lay presenters. (My presenters, Phil and his mother—my mother-in-spirit—Betty Campbell were preparing themselves in other rooms.) Shortly before eleven when the service was to begin, our ordaining bishops came into the room. It was time for the traditional signing of the Oath of Conformity, which each of us in turn read aloud, slowly and thoughtfully, before affixing her signature to it in the presence of her ordaining bishop.

Before any ordination to the diaconate, priesthood, or episcopate, the ordinand is required by the Constitution of the Episcopal Church to sign an oath declaring that she or he will "engage to conform" to the doctrine, discipline, and worship of the Episcopal Church. While many clergy may consider this a mere matter of form, we were painfully aware of our dilemma as the oath was passed among us.

How could we sign this oath with integrity, knowing that we were about to fail in conformity to the discipline of the Episcopal Church by violating a point of canon law? Our breach with the letter of the law was in our inability, in most cases, to obtain the recommendations of our Standing Committees or diocesan bishops. But each of us felt convinced in her heart that we were doing so in order to conform with the Church's teaching of wholeness in Christ. In other words, we failed to conform to discipline because discipline failed to conform to doctrine, and since discipline is the interpreter and enabler of doctrine as the teaching of Christ, it is constantly in process and subject to change according to our growing understanding. Conflict among doctrine, discipline, and worship is inevitable, and anyone who makes that oath honestly and thoughtfully faces the fact that there will be times when she or

127

he will violate it in good conscience, and in fidelity to the living process (and its creative conflict) of our growing understanding of Christ's teaching.

Ours was a case in which, as women, disobedience of the letter of the law was the only way in which we could express our obedience to the Spirit of Christ. The only way for us to be spared the conflict of this predicament would have been for our Standing Committees and diocesan bishops to accept our qualifications for the priesthood as human persons, rather than to have disqualified us on first sight only because of our womanhood. Since this did not happen, we had to assume the authority to claim Christ's calling for ourselves, and in community with persons who recognized this calling, rather than those whose prejudicial interpretation of the law blinded them to the legitimate claim that Christ had upon us for the Church.

During the service, Bishop Corrigan read this statement that expressed our common position regarding the Oath of Conformity:

> Our common dilemma is presented at the outset by the requirement that each ordinand, first, declare her belief that the Holy Scriptures of the Old and New Testaments contain all things necessary to salvation; secondly, take the canonical Oath of Conformity to the doctrine, discipline, and worship of the Protestant Episcopal Church in the United States of America; and thirdly, make a similar liturgical promise placed in the ordinal.
>
> The conflict between both revelation in the scriptures and the doctrine of the Church, on the one hand, and the discipline, rules and regulations and common practices of the Protestant Episcopal Church on the other hand, have long been both observed and experienced.

There is nothing new in being compelled to choose the truth revealed in scripture and expressed in doctrine when this truth is in conflict with our rules and ways.

This is such a time. Neither the Word nor the great exposition of that Word forbid [sic] what we propose. Indeed, that which both declare about women in creation and in the new creation command [sic] our present action. The time for our obedience is now.

Clearly, our position reflected the teaching and example of Christ in the gospels with regard to women, rather than the countless contradictory cultural references about the expected roles of women scattered through the pseudo-Pauline pastoral letters, or even some of Paul's own correspondence. Paul, like the rest of us, grew and changed, and we can find instances of him changing his mind about women, as he separated his own enculturation from the teaching of Christ. We, after all, are like Paul in that we, too, grow and change, and we, too, are not *Paul*ians, but *Christ*ians. Likewise, the place of women in the old dispensation reflected the exclusivity of a patriarchal religion, a sin from which Christ redeemed us in the new dispensation, of which we are *equal heirs*.

We were not alone in holding this position, for nearly two thousand people awaited our ordinations inside the Church of the Advocate—an astounding thing when you consider that the event had limited publicity beforehand.

As we stood behind the sanctuary with the other ordinands and our priest and lay presenters, we heard spontaneous laughter and then applause coming from inside the church. The sound was our first clue that there was a mighty and joyous throng on the other side to meet us and celebrate with us. One of us asked what had happened to arouse such a response. We were told that Paul Washington, the rector, had welcomed the people. He commented that everyone present was participating in a *kairotic*[1] moment in time, and that it is not always possible to predict or determine history in advance. Then he gave an illustration that went something like this: If the Church Fathers still claimed that women's time had not yet come in the Church, they should take note that, even though her obstetrician tells a woman that she will give birth on August 15, if the baby is coming on July 29, it is the woman and the baby who are right, not the obstetrician. It was at this point that we heard the congregation's loud affirmation. Then the opening hymn was announced: "Come Labor On!" Indeed, our time *had* come.

Early in the service, Dr. Charles Willie delivered the sermon, as was truly fitting for him to do. The Anglican Communion until recently has, for a good many years, been bilingual in its worship. While the Prayer Book liturgy was spoken in majestic Elizabethan English, sermons were usually delivered in contemporary dialect appropriate to the region—in our case, some form of American. We preserved this fine old tradition in our ordination service by using the 1928 (virtually the 1662) version of the Book of Common Prayer, while inviting an eloquent contemporary American to preach the sermon. Dr. Willie's moving rhetorical style was in the finest preaching tradition. His powerful utterance was filled with the Holy Spirit. I saw him that day as the charismatic champion of ecclesiastical rights in the same way that Dr. Martin Luther King, Jr., had been the champion of civil rights. These are his words, on "The Priesthood of All Believers":

"The hour cometh and now is when the true

---

[1] *Kairos:* the moment of life-changing opportunity and decision, perceived as the depth dimension of eternity breaking through into the linear dimension of time, God's moment of self-revelation in our lives, when *all things come together.*

worshippers shall worship God in spirit and in truth."

This is the hour of truth. As Martin Buber would describe it: This is a living moment of truth which stands between creation and redemption. But let us not make too much over it, because Martin Buber also tells us that "creation . . . takes place . . . [not only at the beginning but] at every moment throughout the whole of time," and that "redemption . . . takes place . . . [not only at the end but] at every moment throughout the whole of time." So let us not make too much of this hour, for "we live in an unredeemed world."

Nevertheless, there is reason to rejoice in the face of the deep human sorrow which we cause. We have come together as part of the continuing process of creation. And we hope that our actions will be a contribution toward the continuing process of redemption. Moreover, we believe as Buber has said, that "out of each human life that is unarbitrary and bound to the world, a seed of redemption falls into the world and the harvest is God's."

May God bless the harvest of this moment, so that it will not be a high moment in the history of the Episcopal Church but a holy moment in time. Because things more important than my remarks will happen during this hour I will be brief.

First, may I make a few statements as an introduction. I participate in this service today not because I wanted to speak out but because I could not remain silent. Also, I should like to make it perfectly clear that I speak neither as an officer of the Church nor as a professor of any school but as a child of God who has decided to make no peace with oppression.

Finally, I stand ready to suffer the consequences of my actions, knowing, as Martin Luther King often said, that unearned suffering is redemptive. And so I wish to talk with you awhile about the priesthood of all believers.

Four years ago at the 1970 General Convention in Houston the Committee on Theological Education urged the House of Deputies to adopt a resolution affirming "that women are eligible to seek and accept ordering ... to the priesthood and to be ordained and consecrated to the episcopate." May I remind you of the vote on that resolution.

As you know, a deputation to General Convention consists of eight people—four clergy and four lay people. When a vote by orders is called for, the clergy and lay people vote separately. Under the rules of vote by orders there are only two votes per deputation—one for all clergy and one for all lay people. Of the 99 clerical deputations that voted in Houston, 49.7 per cent favored the ordination of women and 29.0 per cent were against; 21.2 per cent were split, with some clergy favoring and some opposing ordination [to the priesthood and episcopate]. Among lay people, there were 91 deputations that voted; 54.1 per cent favored the ordination of women, while 31.6 per cent were against; only 14.3 per cent of the deputations of lay people were split, with some favoring and some opposing. Of all deputations that voted for or against the ordination of women in Houston, therefore, clearly a majority favored their ordination. But the wish of the majority was frustrated because of an archaic practice in the Episcopal Church of counting a deputation which is split or divided as a negative vote, even though some members in a divided deputation

132

wish an issue to be favorably considered. It should go without saying that such a method of voting is undemocratic. How can the church counsel the state on ways of perfecting democracy when the Church's own methods of decision-making are defective?[2]

Some women who believe that they have been called to be priests in the Episcopal Church in the United States were disappointed by this legal but undemocratic action in 1970. But they waited believing that in 1973, as Martin Luther King, Jr., used to say, "the rough places [would be] made plains, and the crooked places . . . made straight." But such was not to be. In 1973, the Louisville General Convention passed into history without acting favorably upon any resolution affirming the right of women to be ordained as priests.[3]

Twice during the 1970 decade the General Convention was presented the opportunity to confirm the personhood of women by affirming their right to be professional priests. Twice did it blunder. Some might say that the actions of General Convention were not sexist and had nothing to do with discrimination against women. But I say that an overwhelming majority of the General Convention members are men. This fact speaks louder than their denial of the presence of prejudice.

An article by two male reporters in the *Conven-*

---

[2] I have heard this question answered, "Because the Church doesn't need democracy—it has the Holy Spirit! We don't need human justice because divine justice will win out no matter what we do." Isn't this avoiding responsibility and *tempting God?*

[3] It's been said that priesthood isn't a matter of rights. This is very true. No one has a right to the priesthood, but men have had the *right to respond to God's call* to the priesthood, while women have not.

tion Daily summarizing the actions of the 1973 General Convention made this observation:

"If you are a woman interested in ordination to the priesthood or episcopacy you will have to wait awhile. And no one knows for how long."

There is a dictum in American jurisprudence that justice delayed is justice denied.

The General Convention continued a sexist policy of refusing to recognize the priesthood of all believers by not affirming the right of women to be professional priests.[4] This it did after "the triennium of the women of the Church had overwhelmingly urged the Convention to make them eligible for full pastoral roles in the Church. . . . " Such political action by General Convention flying in the face of such moral persuasion is an affront to the personhood of women and prompts a rhetorical question: How long, how long, O God, must a good woman wait? How much, how much, O God, can a good woman take?

There are parallels between the Civil Rights Movement and the Women's Movement and this is what we are witnessing today. In reality, both are freedom movements for men as well as women, and for blacks and browns as well as whites. Unfulfilled hope tends to turn into despair and eventually into rage. You recall the end of the 1960 decade and how frustrated blacks were enraged. "Back in 1963 there

---

[4] The priesthood is said to represent Christ to the people and the people to Christ. I've addressed myself earlier in the last chapter to the ability of women to represent Christ as baptized persons and priests. Until now, lay women have had no one symbolizing their priesthood to them, for the male priest alone was said to symbolize and represent all humanity. This may be true in an integrated priesthood when women and men can both and each represent the community, but it's not true in an exclusive priesthood.

134

was hope. Louis Harris found that nearly two-thirds of black Americans believed that the attitudes of whites would be better in about five years. But in 1968, five years later, that hope had not been fulfilled. As a matter of fact, the gap between whites and blacks was widening in some areas, and in 1968 the esteemed leader of poor black people, the Rev. Dr. Martin Luther King, Jr., was assassinated." [From Dr. Willie's book, *Church Action in the World*, Morehouse-Barlow, 1969.]

Rioting broke out in over 100 communities across the nation. These were the actions of enraged people full of despair, without hope, who couldn't take any more at that time.

Now we see in our Church that some members are in a condition of defiance similar to the defiance against the state which occurred in the Civil Rights Movement. The hope after Houston for the full participation of women in the Church was dashed in Louisville and two men reporters said "no one knows for how long."

And so we who believe in the priesthood of all believers have experienced an injustice perpetrated by the Convention of the Church which we love.

The responsibility now falls directly upon those who feel aggrieved "to make no peace with oppression," and to redeem the General Convention from a foolish mistake. And we stand ready to endure the hardship and the personal sacrifice necessary to pull the Episcopal Church from its mistaken way of refusing to acknowledge the full personhood of women by denying them full participation in the priesthood.

As blacks refused to participate in their own oppression by going to the back of the bus in 1955 in Montgomery, women are refusing to cooperate in their own oppression by remaining on the periphery of full participation in the Church in 1974 in Philadelphia. It was an unjust law of the state that demeaned the personhood of blacks by requiring them to move to the back of the bus, and it is an unjust law of the Church which demeans women by denying them the opportunity to be professional priests. Since the state and the Church steadfastly refused to rectify these wrongs in an orderly way, self-determination now is in order. We will break the law of the Church and we will suffer the consequences knowing that unearned suffering is redemptive.

How can a religious organization condemn sexism in the world and at the same time condone legislative action which discriminates against women in the Church? We have come here today to secure the rights of full participation. If it must be done, 'tis better that it be done now.

Psychiatrist Robert Seidenberg has observed, "The era of passive acceptance of inequality as well as feminine obeisance is rapidly coming to an end." It is because of this and the refusal of the General Convention to act while there was yet time, that this moment is upon us. We must be careful, however, to celebrate it not as an event of arrogant disobedience but as a moment of *tender loving defiance.* [My italics.] The theologian Martin Buber has said that "dogmas and rules are merely the result ... of the human mind's attempt to make comprehensible ... the working of the unconditional." Our contemporary image of the priesthood as consisting of men only is our humble and limited comprehension of how that which is known should be related to the unknown. Buber tells us that "time after time, the image must be broken, the iconoclasts must have their way." He

136

calls the iconoclasts the soul of humankind "which rebels against having an image that can no longer be believed in, elevated above the heads of [people] as a thing that demands to be worshipped." He goes on to say that "the commandment, 'Thou shalt not make unto thee an image' ... does not ... refer merely to sculptored or painted images, but to our fantasy, to all the power of our imagination as well. [People are] forced time and again to make images, and forced to destroy them when [they] realize [they have] not succeeded." And so we live in an unredeemed world [one that has not embraced redemption], in many respects not unlike the kind of world into which Jesus came. He shattered the images of his time, was crucified, but continues to live. In the world in which we live today, filled with war, crime, and injustice, obviously the image of a male priesthood has not been successful. Why does it deserve to remain?

Let no one confuse the work of the General Convention with the will of God and the unconditional. They may or may not be the same. Moreover, Buber has said that "human truth can be communicated only if one throws oneself into the process and answers for it with oneself."

And so we throw ourselves into this process because we believe in love and we believe in justice and we believe in the Scriptures and we believe it is a Christian duty to disobey unjust laws. No longer are some women willing to cooperate in their own oppression. Psychiatrist Seidenberg states that "it seems inconceivable that in the future women will be shut out as they have been in the past. The new militancy with its demands for justice and fair play appears undaunted," he said.

What we are doing is in the best of biblical

tradition. "In the earliest known social pattern of ancient Israel priests as a class did not exist." A special intercessor to present offerings to God was not necessary. Thus "the concept of Israel as a nation of priests" was established and is recorded in the Book of Exodus (9:5-6). The priestly caste came later in Israel's life. Then the thought is advanced in Revelation (1:6, 5:10) that "Christian believers and their Church are 'kings and priests' unto God." This is the idea of the priesthood of all believers. [Dr. Willie cites his source: *Harper's Bible Dictionary,* revised, Harper and Row, 1973, pp. 578, 580.]

"The women's struggle, like many others," [says Seidenberg] "is not a battle of good against evil but a conflict of diverse forms each of which has a legitimate claim to be heard." The General Convention is the only mechanism we have in the Episcopal Church for gaining the consensus of all members through deputies whom they dispatch to meetings every three years. As such, it is a delicate means of achieving collegial authority and this is something of value. It should be said that affirming the personhood of men and women and their right to participate in society and its institutions is something of value, too. And this right also must be guarded and guaranteed. The affirmation of personhood and full participation of women in the Church has been ignored for too long in favor of collegiality and the authority of corporate intransigence. When two claims—the right to full participation in society and its institutions and the right to maintain a system of corporate authority—are in contention, a choice is necessary. In my system of values, the right of persons takes precedence over the right of corporations when the two are in contention with each other, especially when the right of one person does not

138

interfere with the right of another. It is time the Church recognized that it is the servant of its members. The purpose of law, including church law, is to enhance humanity of men and women and boys and girls. A law which demeans personhood is a law unworthy of obeying.

At a time like this, we think of words like these, written by James Russell Lowell more than 100 years ago:

> Once to every [one] and nation
> Comes the moment to decide
> In the strife of truth and falsehood
> For the good or evil side . . .
> Then it is the brave [one] chooses
> While the coward stands aside
> 'Til the multitude makes virtue
> Of the faith they had denied . . .
> New occasions teach new duties,
> Time makes ancient good uncouth;
> They must upward still and onward
> Who would keep abreast of truth.

God grant that the Church may see the true mission of women as it is meant to be. Here we stand to stake our claim and our version of truth as we understand it, that all believers are priests in the kingdom of God and have a right to fully participate in the affairs of Church and society. And we also vow to make no peace with oppression, whether it is sexism or racism. We can do nothing else so help us God. With God's help we shall overcome. Amen.

After the sermon, a time had been provided for orderly protest. Several male priests came up into the chancel to read prepared statements. All but the last were self-controlled and

139

dignified. The last priest was a young man who appeared to be emotionally distraught. He shook his fist at the ordaining bishops, shouting, "Sirs, you will never again be called bishops, for today you violate the law of God that says *his* priests shall be called *Father*." Phil whispered to me the words of Jesus, "Call no man Father." The young priest went on: "You are trying to turn stones into bread." After likening us to stones and our bishops to Satan, he then suggested that, if human, we were neither adults nor free agents. Still speaking to the bishops he accused: "You are offending these little ones!" Finally, he announced: "Today you break the bond between Adam and Eve." At that moment audible gasps of disbelief were heard throughout the congregation. I heard Phil mutter "Heresy," and my own response was, as I quietly observed to him, that it was high time the bond were broken if it was based on domination and the kind of disrespect we had just witnessed.

Our spirits and our wills were still held high, and the liturgy and the ordinations continued. We shared the Bread of Life together in deepest joy.

As I stood in the sanctuary during Holy Communion, administering the holy food with my sister priests, seeing the radiant faces of those many people who had come to make this moment happen with us, many things came together in my heart. I remembered the words of Jeremiah, and then the words of Jesus to the dead daughter of Jairus, calling her back to life: *Talitha Cumi*, "Young woman, I say to you, arise." And I looked at the beautiful faces of all the women present, reflecting the love and presence of the Holy Spirit. Compared to the light I saw in my sisters' faces, the dark words we had heard a few moments before had no power or truth whatever. These reflections were combining to later become this poem:

Talitha Cumi

"Young woman, I say to you, Arise."

Luke 8:54

140

Do not send me, O God,
for I am only a woman
and do not know what to say.

*Do not say
"I am only a woman."
Rise up a New Creation
and take the name
I Am.*

Am I a stone that my body
should be turned to bread?
Am I a little one whom others
should not offend?
Am I not dumb and immovable
and worse than dead?

*You are being and motion,
fire in the mountain,
storm in the sea-deep,
vermillion sky-gilding sun.
Rise up a New Creation
and take the name
I Am.*

Am I a devil,
a danger,
a soul-dagger-drudge,
a babe,
a hag,
a desert,
a plague?

*You are
a woman
a human*

141

a person
a prophet
a sister
a creature
an icon-breaker/re-maker
a judgment
a vision
a life.

Rise up a New Creation
and take the name

I Am.

I realized that all of us were involved in a movement of
the Holy Spirit that transcended the particular calling of any
individual woman, but included all women together at this
moment in history in a common calling to renew the Church
and the world. Our calling is the calling of Christ the Liberator.
Responding to it requires tremendous courage from us all,
courage that we can only get from each other, and from God
within us. Aware of the collectivity of the healing impact of
women in the Church and the world, I wrote this poem on the
day of our ordinations to the priesthood, to honor all women
seeking wisdom in all parts of the earth, especially in all
communities of faith:

Call

There is a new sound
of roaring voices in the deep
and light-shattered rushes in the heavens.
The mountains are coming alive,
the fire-kindled mountains
moving again to reshape the earth.

142

It is we sleeping women,
waking up in a darkened world,
cutting the chains
from off our bodies with our teeth,
stretching our lives over the slow earth,
seeing, moving, breathing in the vigor
that commands us to make all things new.

It has been said that while the women sleep
the earth shall sleep. But listen!
We are waking up and rising,
and soon our sister will know her strength.
The earth-moving day is here.
We women wake to move in fire.
The earth shall be remade.

Our time had come. Not only our time, but woman's time had come, and is still coming in a continuing process of liberation and sanctification.

We had hoped that a consequence of our ordinations would be to draw the issue of women priests out of the speculative arena of the General Convention into the clean air of indisputable reality. We were the *fait accompli* of women in the priesthood.

The question we lived out for the next two years was: Can the Episcopal Church accept us? The question was not only for ourselves, but for all women, and for a whole priesthood. During that time I grew fond of quoting T. S. Eliot's Becket: "Humankind cannot bear very much reality." We women are real. We are beginning to be borne, but there is yet much about us that a sinful society and a sexist Church must learn to bear well.

143

Controversy

The House of Bishops did not accept our reality at all.

Two weeks after our ordinations, bishops were called away from their vacations for a special emergency meeting of the House of Bishops at O'Hare Inn in Chicago. Most of the women priests gathered together nearby to pray for the bishops and to be available should any of them want to speak with us. None did. There was panic and pandemonium in the House of Bishops.

As we women waited things out in Sue Hiatt's room in another motel, we talked over the possibilities of the bishops' reactions. It was Sue, who always sensed the awful truth in a bad situation before any of the rest of us, who said "I think they'll declare us invalid." And it was I who retorted, "Impossible! They can't do that."

But they did it, angry enough to change the theological definition of validity to do so. Whether it was anger or political expediency or both that was responsible, that is exactly what they did. In a confused session late in the afternoon, the bishops cast their votes on validity. After the vote was counted, one of the bishops addressed the chair, asking, "Could you please tell us what we just voted on? Many of us don't know!" When the Presiding Bishop told him that they had voted to declare the "event" invalid and women priests

144

non-existent, many bishops changed their votes from "Yes" to "No," and some then abstained. Still, the majority stood in favor of invalidity, contrary to the Church's teaching on the sacrament of ordination.

✳ Validity of ordination depends on the presence of right form (in this case, the ordinal of the Book of Common Prayer), right intention (to make a deacon, priest, or bishop), and right matter (a qualified human being called by God and the Church to that office). Perhaps some actually thought that we were not right matter, since, as women, our being human was questionable! The reasoning given was that we could not be real priests since we had not been ordained in the communities where we were canonically resident. In other words, a canonical irregularity was in this case, and for purely political reasons, confused with sacramental validity.

Theologians reminded the Church and the bishops that the House of Bishops did not have the authority to rewrite the theology of ordination, and that their statement was not legislation, but mere opinion, since they were only one half of a bicameral legislative body. To us, it seemed absurd that the question, "Are women human?" was still being asked, and it embarrassed us that it was being asked by part of our own Church.

For the next two years, the bishops effectively avoided the fact of our existence as women priests. Our priesthood existed all the same, and so did our womanhood. The bishops were telling us that just by *being women* we were outlaws — outside the structure of Church law, therefore, non-existent. Certainly to them we were invisible, and remained so for two years.

The House of Bishops met again in October at their next regularly scheduled meeting, which happened that time to be in Mexico. They modified their August statement by saying that we were "not recognizable but not incompletable." And so the ecclesiastical machinery continued to make judgments

145

about us without any direct contact with us.

On September 7, 1975, four more women deacons were ordained to the priesthood in Washington, D. C. The Rev. Lee McGhee, the Rev. Betty Rosenberg, the Rev. Alison Palmer, and the Rev. Diane Tickell were ordained to the priesthood by the Rt. Rev. George Barrett, retired. The second wave of women priests was as efficiently overlooked by the hierarchy as the first wave had been. Still the fifteen of us went on living out our priesthood in fifteen unique ways, discovering and authenticating in our own lives our participation in the priesthood of Christ and the priesthood of all believers, and learning the consequences of our kairotic moment in time as they gradually unfolded.

After our ordinations to the priesthood, two male priests were tried and found guilty in ecclesiastical courts of disobeying their bishops' "godly admonitions" by inviting women priests to celebrate the Eucharist in their parishes. In fact, they were found guilty of celebrating a whole priesthood by acknowledging women priests. The Rev. Peter Beebe was later declared not guilty by an appellate court, largely on the basis of ambiguity on what constitutes a godly admonition, and of the fact that the diocesan court failed to take into account the validity issue.

Three of our ordaining bishops were censured publicly by their brothers in the House of Bishops, and all of them have been treated publicly and privately as *persona non grata* by their colleagues. As Charles Willie had predicted, they were vilified and talked about, but not physically crucified.

There were two major political action groups that formed after the Philadelphia ordinations, representing the two points of view regarding the political philosophy of the positive side of the issue. The National Coalition for Women in the Priesthood held that it was expedient to work toward clarification through change in canon law, and it therefore directed itself to legislative action at General Convention. The national Women's Ordination Now (WON) group held that since there were already women priests in the Episcopal Church, all that was needed was for the bishops to recognize those priests and for the Church to give thanks to God for bringing this to pass.

The work of the Coalition went full speed ahead into political strategy for the General Convention convening in Minneapolis in the fall of 1976. Much backroom politicking went on as the time approached. Representatives of the major opposition group, the Committee for an Apostolic Ministry (CAM), met with leaders of the Coalition and the Presiding Bishop a few weeks before Convention to discuss options. It appeared to others of us, particularly those involved in WON, that the political compromise achieved behind the scenes was to involve the sacrifice of the fifteen women who were already priests. Clearly, we were troublesome to both the opposition and the "pro" side, for we represented a radical position that didn't mesh well with the Coalition's intent to work through the existing political and legal structures. Some of the "pro" people were as eager as the "con" people to have us out of the way during the tense sessions of the General Convention. Our friends and supporters in WON—who truly believed the issue had *already been won* by our existence—worried that we women priests would be sold down the river in backroom bargaining. The WON people had worked for two years to make the real issue apparent to the Church at large, by supporting public celebrations of the Eucharist by women priests, and by supporting those male priests who were openly and covertly persecuted for their recognition and active support of the priesthood of women, while the women priests were never directly dealt with by the hierarchy.

On September 11, 1976, the opening session of the General Convention began. Several of my sister priests arrived from various parts of the country—one from as far away as Alaska—and we held our own counsel together at the home of Sue Hiatt's mother in Minneapolis and here at Wisdom

147

House. Some of us refused to grant the General Convention any relevance, and for that reason, didn't come. Those of us who were here had various motives—some simply wanted to see the process as it happened; others were here to support our supporters; I myself had resolved some weeks before to have nothing to do with the General Convention. None of us believed that anything positive would happen.

Given the procedural obstacles that I laid out earlier, I had no faith at all that anything different would happen at this Convention. I knew that it would only be self-destructive to subject myself to another life-denying process, so I decided to stay away from what I believed to be an alien space. The priests who were staying with us went faithfully to every session during the first few days of the Convention. On those few occasions when I had to go to Convention headquarters to deliver or pick up something for the local WON committee, my stomach would hurt for an hour. I began to lose weight. I knew that it was not good for me to be there.

The one truly joyous event in which I did actively participate was a Eucharist in Celebration of a Whole Priesthood, which our ordaining bishops were originally invited to concelebrate; but after the invitation was withdrawn by the bishop of Minnesota, the presiding ministers were Bishops Kilmer Myers, Coleman McGehee, and Brooke Mosley. It was a high moment, a festive affirmation of all that the movement for a whole priesthood had stood for, an occasion for strengthening and deepening of faith for all of us. This took place in a downtown church on September 12, Phil's and my fifth wedding anniversary. It was a beautiful way to celebrate. The church was packed with Episcopalian, Roman Catholic, and Protestant supporters from all over the country who were of one mind and one spirit in seeking new wholeness for the Church.

One of the most authentic moments in liturgy I have ever experienced was during that service, when the presiding

148

minister, Bishop Mosley, greeted the congregation with the peace of Christ at the traditional time of the Kiss of Peace. He opened his arms to us and said in a large voice, "Now you all greet each other in whatever way you need to. Seek out the people you need to touch or speak to, and if you need to ask someone's forgiveness, or tell someone how much you value them, do it now. If you need to embrace someone, or shake hands, or just look at each other for a moment, do it now. But make peace with one another in the name of Christ." For fifteen minutes the church was a beehive of reconciliation, affection, appreciation, reunion—the overflowing and lively peace that is not peace as this world knows it, but the extraordinarily active peace of Christ.

It was after this Eucharist for a Whole Priesthood that I went home and began to reflect on the story of the raising of Lazarus, which I had heard during another liturgy some days earlier. I began to connect Lazarus with the Episcopal Church itself, and the result was this poem I wrote for my Church's process during the two weeks of this General Convention. (As you can see, I was not completely without hope. Just as I can't allow myself to be too optimistic, neither can I live without hope.)

Lovesong in the House of Quarrelsome Overseers[1]

Meditation on John 11:17-44

Jesus wept.
The human side we've failed
to worship,
the side of sweat and tears
and jokes and righteous rage
and deep, so deep fatigue.

---

[1] "House of Quarrelsome Overseers" is the literal translation of "Episcopal Church" in Mandarin idiom.

149

Like a mother longing
over the bricks and stones
of Israel's heart.
Like a mother yearning
over the stifling child
choked on its own
dry tongue and spittle.
Jesus wept.

And two sisters rush to the tasks of faith:
remorse, rebuke, rebirth.
We dead entreat you.
Loose us. Let us go.

Stinking, old, despaired of,
Lazarus, come forth.

When I say that I had some small amount of hope for the
General Convention, I don't mean that I thought legislation
was necessary to accomplish our goal of a whole priesthood
and a whole people, but there's no question about the healing
value of a positive political act. The negative side of the
Convention's intervention in the issue was that it implied that
political action was the necessary approval of the humanity and
holiness of women. Clearly many women saw this implication
and were offended by it. The positive side was that its affirmation (rather than approval) of the priesthood of women would
give credence and confirmation to the existing ministries of *all*
women in the Church, and this was certainly desirable.

We women priests were by and large of the opinion that
positive legislative action would in fact be dangerous for
women in the Church, because at that time we were strongly
sensitive to the threat of being co-opted, as women, into a
sexist structure that would not allow us the expression of our
femaleness as ministers (lay or ordained), but would in fact

attempt to absorb us into patriarchy. I was aware of enormous ambivalence in my own feelings about the General Convention. On the one hand, another rejection would be too painful for any of us, especially for the women deacons who were still waiting for the Convention's approval, or at least, for its seeming "legitimization" of their priesthood. On the other hand, a positive response from the Convention could easily lead to co-optation, the easy pacification of women by a Church that was still male-dominated, allowing a few token women into the sacred male ranks of priesthood and episcopacy, but maintaining its misogynist posture toward lay women at the grass roots level.

Phil and I had decided to be out of town on the day of "The Vote." It was scheduled for the end of the first week or beginning of the second week on the agenda, but because everyone was so tense about the priesthood of women issue, several attempts were made to move it up. On Thursday, September 16, Phil and I were making plans for our day off when the phone rang. Katrina Swanson was calling to tell us about a luncheon for clergy couples at the Holiday Inn at noon—Could we come? We decided "Yes," that would be a good thing to do. We could take our day off afterward.

I began to get dressed, starting out with a comfortable, bright long dress that would be cool on this hot day. Phil looked at me and suggested that I might want to appear more clerical for the occasion. I grimaced, but agreeably got out my clerical collar. It did not go well with the bright long dress with its wonderful orange butterflies. It did not go well with the cool, short green dress. I took a look at what Phil was wearing—his best elegant beige suit with brown clergy shirt and clerical collar. He gave me a look back that said, "Stop fooling around and put on your good clergy clothes." Much as I hated to, I got out my own best black jersey pants suit, rabat, and clerical collar ensemble, pinned a black and gold butterfly to my lapel, put up my hair, and completely gave in to what

151

seemed the demands of the occasion. Little did I know what a good thing it was that I had done so.

We arrived at the Holiday Inn a few minutes before noon. Another clergy couple met us at the front door. "The luncheon's been cancelled," the woman told us, "so we could all get good seats for the big vote this afternoon." "You mean it's going to be *today?*" I asked. "Yes. This morning the agenda committee decided to call for it this afternoon."

Phil and I looked at each other. "We've been tricked," I said. "God knew we'd never get here on our own. After all this trouble to get us here, I guess the least we can do is stay. But just for a few minutes!" Phil agreed. As we walked over to Convention Hall, I decided that my presence would be a sign of support to all the WON people who had worked so hard in Minnesota especially over the last two years. And there were so many women deacons there who would need support. I resolved to be there for their sakes, but still, I had no intention of sitting it out for the whole afternoon. I really didn't want to be there when the bad news came.

At two o'clock I was giving back rubs to various persons and words of encouragement to others, when I decided it was probably time for me to leave, before things got too tense. Phil said, "Oh, let's stay a little longer. It's just beginning." At three-thirty, we had already heard forty minutes worth of debate, and nothing new. I was getting anxious about the dinner we were going to put on that evening for the women priests, our ordaining bishops, a group of WON people, and their families. "Phil," I said, "we have to buy groceries for tonight. We'd better go soon."

"Just a little longer," he said. "The vote may come up soon."

"That's what I'm afraid of," I thought to myself.

At five, the debate was still going on. I had decided to take Phil's car and do the shopping myself, leaving Phil to find his way home on his own. Several people I knew stopped me on my way out of the long Convention Hall. I was delayed just long enough for Phil to catch me, followed by Sam Ford, a reporter for the Minneapolis television station WCCO. "Alla," said Phil, "Sam wants to interview you right at 6 o'clock for WCCO's live Action Camera. He says it's really important. I think you should do it." In despair, I looked at my watch, realized I couldn't possibly buy groceries, start dinner, and get back here by six. "All right," I said. "I'll stay."

At five minutes to six, the debates were closed. The presiding officer called for the vote, and asked everyone present first to stand up for five minutes of silent prayer together. At 6 o'clock, the voting began. Sam Ford motioned me down from the visitors' gallery. I stood in front of the voting delegates, and when Sam asked me on live television what I thought the outcome would be, I surprised myself by saying "The power of the prayer we shared together in this room just now can lead to only one thing. The Holy Spirit is among us. The outcome will be positive."

I was even more surprised half-an-hour later when the vote had been tallied and was announced. There was absolute silence in the large, crowded room, as delegates, visitors, and reporters waited to hear the outcome. No one was breathing in my section of the gallery.

The presiding officer read out the tally: "In the clergy order, 113 votes cast, 57 necessary. Yes: 60; No: 38; Divided: 16. In the lay order, 114 votes cast, 58 necessary. Yes: 64; No: 37; Divided: 12. The motion is passed."

"Oh, my God," I breathed as I wrote down the figures. Phil and I reached for each other's hands and nearly broke each other's bones squeezing them together. All around us people were weeping, silently reaching, touching each other. No one spoke. Phil was weeping. I do not remember if I wept, I was so thoroughly stunned. Perhaps I did. If not, I am now, this long time later. How long it takes, sometimes, for things to sink in! Thank you, God, for that moment. Thank you for

153

seeing to it that I was there. I would not want to have missed it. If I didn't say *Thank you* then, I say it now, with all my heart.

At seven, immediately after the final proceedings of the House of Deputies, there was an open press conference in which the women priests were interviewed along with representatives of the Coalition and the local WON committee. The press people were somewhat surprised to find that we priests were not bursting with joy as a result of the vote. I told you of our own fears and ambivalence about the outcome of the General Convention, and besides the fact that we were all in shock, these concerns were still very much with us. We spoke of the sexism that still exists in our Church, and warned that, while this affirmation of the priesthood and episcopacy of women was important and good, in itself it had little bearing on the general suffering and oppression of women in the Church, and it would not unless women and men together dedicated themselves to eliminating sexism from our midst in the long haul of years to come.

At seven-thirty, Diane Tickell, Phil, and I flew through the supermarket with three shopping carts and three lists. At seven-forty, Phil was cooking hamburger in our kitchen, Diane was boiling noodles, and I was preparing a cheese mixture for our hot dish. At seven-forty-five, Bishop DeWitt and Charlie and Pooh Ritchie from national WON arrived. Charlie was vacuuming the kitchen carpet and Bishop DeWitt was playing the guitar and singing "Jamaica Farewell" with Phil at seven-fifty-five, and at eight, Mrs. Corrigan was serving wine to Bishop Corrigan and thirty other people as the hot dish bubbled. We shared a delicious team-effort meal together at eight-thirty, and spent the rest of the evening talking about the future, and sharing our confused feelings of shock, exhaustion, fear, and hope.

It was another beginning. It was also an end. We had some grieving to do together, letting go of the process of the preceding two years that had brought us so close together. We

154

feared for the future, for women in the Church, for ourselves. What would we fifteen do now that we were in danger of becoming legal? None of us wanted to be domesticated by the Church. How were we to maintain our integrity now? Under overt oppression, integrity is a fairly clear matter. From now on, the oppression would be less clear, and so would our integrity. The Church had made us into symbols and prophets of a kind. Now we were going to become ordinary priests. In a sense, we were losing our jobs—certainly we were faced with brand new job descriptions. We would all have to find a way to adjust, each in her own way. We were all, at that point, suffering from battle fatigue. Strong and able to endure hell during the worst onslaughts of war, we collapsed into giddy prostration, even despair, now that the war had been won.

The war, to be sure, was not entirely over for us, even though that evening we were weary enough to forget the immediacy of our own situations. Most people did not realize that what happened at the General Convention had no immediate bearing on the fifteen of us already priests. It was still up to our individual bishops to recognize our priesthood, as it had been since our ordinations. During the second week of the Convention, the House of Bishops raised the issue of regularization of the fifteen, a scene that became the real crisis of the Convention as far as women priests were concerned.

Three options were suggested by the theological committee of the House of Bishops: re-ordination, conditional ordination, and simple regularization or recognition. The first option was discarded almost immediately, since the bishops knew there were no grounds on which they could re-ordain anyone once validly ordained. Conditional ordination has never been heard of before. Conditional baptism refers to baptizing someone who doesn't know whether she or he has been baptized before—a kind of "in case you are not already baptized, I baptize you" procedure. But there were two thousand witnesses to our ordinations. There was no doubt

155

that they happened. On Monday, the bishops were probably tired and feeling ungenerous, especially ungenerous toward these particular fifteen people. They voted to recommend that our diocesan bishops conditionally ordain us.

Our diocesan bishops knew us well enought to realize that we could not submit to conditional ordination with integrity—it would be a betrayal of the communities we have served as priests to suddenly throw doubt on the actuality of our priesthood in such a way, and it would betray what we ourselves knew to be true. Late Monday night, the Minnesota Committee for Women's Ordination Now called an emergency meeting to discern a way of saving the Church from this betrayal of its own priesthood. In the meeting, the Presiding Bishop's words of the opening session were recalled: We must stand for reconciliation. At one in the morning, signs were made to be posted in the House of Bishops: "Conditional Ordination is Not Reconciliation."

On Tuesday, the bishops met again, and resumed their discussion on how to respond to the situation of the fifteen. By the grace of God, no less a miracle than the one on September 16 occurred that afternoon, when the bishops unanimously reversed their decision of the day before, and recommended simple regularization by means of a public recognition of our priesthood, which would have reconciling elements for us and the people of each diocese.

It isn't at all accurate to say that we won, but in a larger sense, the Church did win back some of its own integrity during those weeks. Our own sense of something won was not bound to the single issue of women priests any longer.

What we set out to accomplish in Philadelphia—the opening of the priesthood and episcopacy to women—had been won. But since then our goals had changed. We now sought the broader goal of wholeness for the Church, and were only beginning to reflect on what this meant for each of us. Clearly, this was only a beginning in the long task of reaching our new goal. I and my sisters have begun a serious reflective process on how we can effect its realization in our own ministries.

For me, this reflective process is deepening and ongoing, and it has taken shape for the most part since that historic day of September 16, 1976. I had to face several months of procedural red tape between the end of the General Convention and the recognition of my priesthood on January 6, 1977. It was after that, really, that I began fully to assimilate on a conscious level the meaning of the events of the past three years in my own life. Since the recognition of my priesthood, I have been reclaiming my personal life back from history, relieved that I no longer am being placed in the role of a prophet. Certainly there are those who would place me and my sister priests in the roles of villains, or would gladly help us to be martyrs for the Church, but who would never call us prophets! I'm glad I no longer have to face either the burden of prophecy or the epithet of villain, let alone the threat of martyrdom. God knows it will take me the rest of my life just to absorb and realize all the changes I've undergone during these few, but most important, years of my life.

When I went to Philadelphia in 1974, I was dimly aware that the event of our ordinations was a prophetic moment in Christian history, but I perceived it only as a breakthrough for the Church, and had no idea of the dramatic and long-playing controversy that was to follow in its wake. I have never enjoyed controversy for its own sake, and finding myself at the center of it for months and years has not been pleasant. Perhaps I would have given up long ago if the struggle were merely a personal one. I recognized the struggle not as one woman's or fifteen women's quest for recognition, but as the growing pains of our whole household of faith in a new phase of Christian life together. For the sake of my sisters and brothers, I had to stay with the struggle, just as I saw them staying with it for my sake, and for each other's. Through this

157

community-building process, I came to understand not only the liberation movements, but priesthood itself in a different light.

Before my ordination to the priesthood, I viewed priesthood as a sacramental ministry. Now I view it as a sacramental way of life. I have long pondered Jacques Maritain's statement that poetry is ontology, and in the gradual fusion of poetry and priesthood in my own life, I've come to the realization that priesthood is ontology too. Priesthood is a way of *being*, as poetry is a way of *being*. For me, poetry is a receptive and creative way of being in the world; priesthood is a consecrative and iconic way of being in the world. I have come to experience priesthood as a sacramental way of being alive. I believe that this is the meaning of the priesthood of God's people: it is a way of life which re-cognizes the holy and constantly offers it back to God. Poetry and priesthood are two rhythms of recognition that, in my own life, move together as a way of being present to the holy, of acknowledging the holiness of all that is, and of helping others to grow in awareness of the holy, of their own holiness. As poet and priest, I seek to reveal and celebrate the holy forms of God's creation, and to share them with others.

By holiness I mean something akin to what is inexpressible and precious in life, the final deep-down mystery and uniqueness of each living being, and the revelation of that mystery and uniqueness in relationships. As a poet, my vocation is to help others to realize their own poetry, their own ability to make meaningful creations out of their lives; as a priest, my calling is to be truly present to others as a symbol of their own priesthood, their ability to see and to consecrate to God what is holy within our personal and corporate lives.

The main purpose of the ordained priest is to be a living symbol of the whole community's priesthood, re-calling the whole community to its sacrifice of praise. Priesthood is more than the ritual performance of sacrificial acts, or the priest

158

would merely be a functionary requiring no particular charisma or preparation for service in the community. I think that ordination means a certain yielding of the self to a particular way of being: a pastoral way of being for deacons, a sacramental way of being for priests. This yielding of the self is not so much a surface ego-identification with a role or function, but the actual engagement of the person in a symbolic life, which then becomes informed by a unique personality. This becomes the way in which the ordained person's life is no longer merely her or his own, but a life for others.

My own commitment to priesthood expresses my willingness to live a life that is no longer just my own, because I've allowed it (myself) to become a visible symbol, an icon, for others of this dimension of their own lives. I rejoice to be able to do this as a woman, for womanhood has not openly participated in the priestly side of our corporate life. For this reason, I call myself *womanpriest,* showing forth the womanly side of priesthood, redeeming what has been lost or lacking, and proclaiming it good and holy.

I do not suggest that we priests who are women will bring a "feminine sensibility" to priesthood, but that we bring with us our female experience, a perspective and appreciation for human life that comes directly from our existential reality as women.

The sacramentality of life is the way in which the invisible becomes visible, spirit takes form, the unheard speaks forth into our lives. These are the outward signs of inward graces, present to us and surrounding us all the time. The Eucharist, as the primary sacrament among Christians, is the central point of all sacramentality.

As presiding minister of the Eucharist, the Great Thanksgiving of the Christian Church, the priest calls the community together to share in an outward act charged with inward vitality and meaning. When bread is broken and wine is blessed in Christ's name, everyone present participates. When we eat

159

the Bread of Life and drink from the Cup of Healing we celebrate the freedom we share in Christ. But Eucharist extends beyond its own time and place into all times and places, so that the Eucharistic community, the community that recognizes the sacrament of life and healing within the bread and wine, shows forth that celebration in relationships and in all creation.

Every human relationship becomes a sacrament when it is experienced as the outward manifestation of inward graces that overflow into life with others. Ecology would be a sacrament if we approached all creatures and all forms upon the earth as sacred and worthy of our reverence for their own sakes, outward signs of life and motion within them. This sacramental attitude, an attitude in which to meet other beings with reverence, is the essence of the priestly life as I see it.

As James Forest says, priesthood

> is an essential art, an ability to show the rest of us that strawberries and us and planet and spider's web and the invention of such words as love and mercy all have to do with—what phrase to use?—the Lord of the flowers, Yahweh, the presence we know as love, as the deep fear-erasing appetite for justice, the capacity to forgive. It is an extraordinary art to break open the blindness we've inherited. To awaken hope, to give new depth and distance to imagination. To join us to past and possible. To make evident the essence of bread and wine, of water, of syllable, color, hunger, feast. A priest is a guide into essence.

Malcolm Boyd describes the relational dimension of the art of priesthood:

> My feeling is that a priest must be less and less a privileged member of an elite corps, more and more

160

a brother/sister in an open community. Priesthood itself cannot be a cause of separation between people, but rather unity. So priesthood must be continuously validated in life, discovered anew in relationship with other people.

If women clergy in the past were "set aside" by the institutional Church, male clergy were "set above." Now the dichotomy between clergy and laity can only be dissolved if the laity reclaims its priesthood and if clergy reclaim their personhood. The old false categories of the clergy as active and male and of the laity as passive and female are reprehensible. Such assumptions represent a distortion of maleness and femaleness and a gross misapprehension of our unity in Christ. Both baptized ministers (laity) and ordained ministers (clergy) are *laos*, are God's *people*.

The class barrier between clergy and laity is the most prominent problem associated with clericalism. (Another symptom of clericalism is, ironically, the oppression of parochial clergy by laity who treat them as slaves or hirelings without needs or feelings of their own, a situation sometimes fostered by a too cool mystique on the side of the ordained, and sometimes fostered by reactionism on the part of oppressed parochial laity. The result in either case is desperate loneliness and isolation.) The inclusion of women into the ordained priesthood will not automatically eliminate the problem, but the turbulent conditions of our inclusion do provide possibilities of transformation in the spiritual and power structures of the ministry of the Church. Women must seize this opportunity to bring more humane models for ministry into our professional situations, offering alternative styles of ministry to our brothers. This is possible not because of our femaleness, but because our coming constitutes a radical change, thus creating a certain healthy chaos that holds potential for the development of new forms.

161

My own model-making process has led me to a shift in self-definition. I've come to identify myself as a Christian first, and Episcopalian second. I no longer identify myself with the Episcopal Church per se, but with worshipping communities of faith wherever I find them. I am no longer concerned with my role vis-à-vis an ecclesiastical hierarchy, but with my responsible interaction with other persons as we grow together toward human wholeness in our communities. The struggle of the past years has been a gift because it has forced me to re-evaluate my life in relationship to Christian ministry and to the rest of the human community, in and out of the Church. I can't imagine my life now without the challenge to create and define ministry uniquely. Falling unquestioningly into a conventional mode of ministry now seems to me limiting and lustreless compared with the excitement and richness I've found seeking through new structures the God "whose service is perfect freedom."

The freedom to create is also the challenge to take risks and it requires the accompanying courage to make mistakes. I have made my share of mistakes through my own process. I have learned from them, but I shall doubtless continue to make new mistakes, since they are inevitable in growth and human relations. Most of my mistakes have been errors in judgment with regard to media exposure, for I've been too unguarded and spontaneous in sharing the perceptions of a given moment, which can then easily be extracted from context in a whole process that usually includes the opposite dynamic: joy as well as sorrow, hope as well as hurt, faith in spite of anger. As for risks—what is life without risks? Our major concern has to be with the consequences of our actions or decisions in the lives of others. It's one thing to risk all for oneself, but I think we have very little right to take risks that will affect others who may not be involved in our vision or commitment. That's where the issue of risk-taking becomes truly sensitive.

An area involving a degree of risk in the Women's Movement within the Churches is in the ecumenical dynamics of our shared vision and the acting out of that vision. Perhaps the ecumenical dimension of our shared experience is our gift to the Church of a living witness to our oneness in God. While our brother theologians have talked softly about ecumenical relations for years, we women, in actualizing our theology, have realized ecumenism in living out our quest together. The risk is in our plunge into reality, for we must always bear in mind the integrative, reflective side of our process along with the factual.

Ecumenically speaking, we women are not scandalized, as the ecclesiastical bureaucracies still are, by Christians from different traditions worshipping together. We do it spontaneously, joyously, and out of necessity, finding ourselves more genuinely in communion with one another than with the bureaucratic structures that have rejected our gifts as women. We affirm our oneness in Christ and our oneness with each other as women, daughters of God and sisters one to another. Across the lines of denominational boundaries, we ask ourselves the question, "Am I my sister's sister?" Overwhelmingly, the response is "Yes." It must be so, or there is no hope, no future for women in the world.

Men are by no means turned away from this process. We welcome the support and participation of our brothers, not wanting to reject others as we have been rejected, though recognizing that the participation of men must be appropriate to their own and our self-actualization and co-redemption, and for the common good.

One of my most moving experiences in the ecumenical dimension of the Liberation Movement within the Churches came about indirectly (as frequently happens) as a result of the oppression itself. I had been invited to preach on the theme of Liberation Theology, opening a month-long series on Liberation at a Roman Catholic university center. The theme was ritualized in a beautiful Eucharistic liturgy. The (male) Roman Catholic priest and I entered the sacred space together in the midst of the worshipping community. Standing near the front of the congregation were an Episcopal priest and about twelve Episcopalians from the university Episcopal center. The Episcopal bishop of that diocese, hearing in advance of my scheduled coming into his diocese, had forbidden all Episcopal churches, missions, and centers to allow me physically to set foot on Episcopal Church property. The only way for the Episcopal university community to be with me in this town was for them to come to the Roman Catholic community where I had been invited to speak as liberation theologian, and where my priesthood and my womanhood were equally recognized and celebrated by and with the worshipping community. The situation itself was an illustration of the theme, for, as I said in the homily, freedom always costs something, can never just be given but must be actively sought and taken, and is always attached to human values: it is something dear, noble, sacred, and beyond all price. The meaning of freedom in Christ was especially sacred and valuable that night, when Episcopalians received Holy Communion from an Episcopal woman priest at a Roman Catholic liturgy. Later in an informal talk with the community, I told them of my former bigotry, and of how I had once said, "If there are ever women priests in the Episcopal Church, I'm going to Rome." Together we laughed and pondered the divine irony of it: yes, there were women priests in the Episcopal Church, and yes, I had come to Rome—as an Episcopal woman priest! The icon of ecumenism that formed that night as two priests—a woman and a man, an Episcopalian and a Roman Catholic—shared the peace of Christ at the same altar, extending it to our gathered communities sharing the same space; the power of that image will never leave me. I will draw strength and meaning from it for the rest of my life. Others were similarly affected.

Later, because of unwarranted publicity, our worship together became a national ecumenical incident, involving six bishops in a confusion of apologies. They were apparently bound by their positions to stand for Christian apartness and polite protocol rather than to celebrate moments of oneness in Christ. Though our action stirred up controversy once again, it also created a sense of hope among those, including myself, for whom it was a moving sign of wholeness to come.[1]

The ecumenical dimension of our experience contains many of the tensions of the liberation process. They are tensions of transition, brought about by the conflict between present realities and future goals that always interact upon each other, for change occurs as the future is realized in, and becomes, the present.

---

[1] A key question for me is: Can women be Christian? If Christianity is chiefly a patriarchal religion of usurpation, the answer is No. If it is chiefly a religion of love and wholeness then the answer is Yes. Each woman must judge whether or not she can stay in the Church effectively without being diminished or destroyed by it. This is a question I live daily.

Christian Feminism

We are women in transition in a Church in transition. We are constantly caught between the old and the new, between achieving equality of Christian responsibility under the old definitions, and defining ourselves under completely new standards. Through this expansive and difficult process, we do not share the same perspective. We do not necessarily share the same values or goals with regard to ministry itself. I can only speak for myself, and the views that I express reflect my own process, which is different from that of my sister priests, deacons, and lay women in their individual situations. We each have a unique angle of vision, with which each woman informs the total process of re-building the Church, a process that is shared by all.

When I reflected on the collective, historical nature of my personal calling to serve God, the Church, and the world as a priest, I referred back to the women of the Bible. I want to stress again and again that, even though our process of liberation and renewal comes out of our shared efforts and consciousness, our experience can be authentic in terms of the whole task only if we maintain contact with the wisdom of the ages. We draw courage and wisdom not only from one another, but from the great lineage of wise holy women who have gone before us in the faith. A feminist theology must be built on the foundation of the past as well as the reality of the present and the promise of the future. Our theologizing as women is part of a vast continuum that includes the sacred energies of the hidden women of history, as well as the great women of God whom we know through the ages: the prophets and judges of Israel who were women; the apostles and evangelists of New Testament times who were women; and theologians through history such as Catherine of Siena and Teresa of Avila who were doctors of the Church; spiritual geniuses such as Julian of Norwich and Margaret Mary Alacoque; and the countless women, ancient and modern, who precede us in religious renewal in *all* communities of faith. These are the true founders and foremothers of Christian feminism—even those women before and beyond Judeo-Christian culture whose exemplary devotion, wisdom, and sensitivity affect us in a positive way, to both teach and heal us as women of faith.

Christian feminism is alive in all the Churches today, even if feebly, incoherently, or covertly. Women in every tradition are now beginning to examine the religious institutions that have informed our own religious experience, and in which we perceive the need for radical—back to the roots—change and renewal. We are also beginning to take responsibility for bringing that change and renewal to reality.

Some of the superficial aspects of the process reflect deeper symbols of corporate religious life. The common and seemingly preposterous question, "Do we call you Father?" suggests the unthinking relationship we have with our own sexuality, and which our sexuality has with our religious structures. I haven't changed my sex or renounced my femaleness by assuming a way of life formerly identified with males. I've merely expanded that way of life—and redefined it—by bringing femaleness to it, by fulfilling the human qualifications for priesthood *as a woman*.

Another question frequently asked is "What unique

things will women bring to the priesthood?" I object to the suggestion which follows, that women will bring the supposedly "feminine" qualities of compassion, intuition, gentleness, caring, and so on, when in fact these are human qualities visible in persons of both sexes. This suggestion is an insult to male priests who have these gifts, without which ministry could hardly function. Women's contribution to the wholeness of priesthood is not in bringing these gifts to it for the first time, but perhaps in showing that what we've labeled "feminine" and "masculine" are in fact human qualities accessible to all, thus helping men to be more comfortable with many of these characteristics in themselves. Women are as capable of cruelty as men are of compassion, and our only hope of wholeness is in our shared recognition of what is truly human in all of us.

Each woman brings to the priesthood exactly what each man brings: a *self,* uniquely created in the image of God. The wholeness that we bring to the priesthood is in making available to it greater diversity of gifts to the glory of God and for the good of the Church. This diversity isn't dependent on sexual differences alone, for we are all different from another in a thousand ways, and the degree of maleness and femaleness in each one of us makes us unique, not flattened out in a two-way sameness that traps us forever in unholy stereotypes. The wholeness of the priesthood reflects the wholeness of God's people, which is now shown to include women as well as men, one sex no more than the other, but each equally valuable in the sight of God.

I reject the title "Father" not only on the obvious grounds of my gender, but because I no longer believe that the priest should be locked into a paternal/maternal role. Sometimes the priest can be a spiritual mother or father, but to emphasize these relational modes to the exclusion of sister, brother, friend, or guide, is a distortion and limitation of the richness of relationship that can be developed within the Christian community's ministries. I do not want to be a dominating matriarch any more than I want to be a patriarchal priest (God save us from female patriarchs!), for domination has no place in Christ's ministry or in human relationships based on love, freedom, and justice.

Another sign of tensions in the current transitional period is how people are affected by a clerical collar. Many people are shocked and some are repelled at their first sight of a woman in a clerical collar. I believe that this is due to the straightforward strangeness and unfamiliarity of it. People were similarly affected when women began to wear slacks in public. Now women's styles include such variety that no one is surprised to see us dressed in pantsuits. They're just as "feminine" as dresses because people are used to seeing them on females. The clerical collar isn't a male symbol just because only men have worn it in the past, any more than slacks are male symbols. It is wrong to identify a style or a function with one group of people just because that group constitutes the majority of its adherents.

My own feelings about the clerical collar, besides finding it an uncomfortable article of clothing, go in two directions. On the one hand, if it limits a relationship by creating an image of separateness and aboveness inappropriate to ministry, if it is a sign to others of hierarchical detachment, institutional coldness, impersonalism and exclusivity, then I shun it, as I shun anything that interferes with the possibility of open, warm, personal encounters between human beings. The clerical collar must be rejected if it defeats the purposes of ministry rather than enhancing them. I do not believe that it should be worn, for example, to inspire fear of authority in "awestruck amateurs" (the people in the pew), or to be treated deferentially by police officers or tax collectors! On the other hand, to many people the clerical collar is an instant identification of "someone who cares." I believe that it should be worn if one can prejudge that the other person will take it as a sign that

169

someone representing the Christian community cares. I wear my collar when I visit the sick in hospitals, or the elderly in nursing homes, because in most cases there it is a positive and immediate sign of caring. For the moment, it's also a strong positive sign to many women, who see a woman in a clerical collar as a sign of their own significance in a Church that really does consider that women count and are important people, contrary to the message conveyed in the past. Perhaps some kind of new physical symbol is needed for both men and women in ordained ministry. It will take time to create new and appropriate symbols, free of the unfortunate double meaning of the collar. This is one of the difficulties of transition. I don't know of a way to transit gracefully other than by being sensitive to the ambiguities and trying to respond to them appropriately in each situation.

Since there are no female models for priestly ministry, we women are creating our own models as we go. This means constantly having to ask ourselves, "Am I copying a male stereotype inappropriately, or am I creating ministry out of this unique situation and relationship?" It's easy to become confused, to find ourselves unconsciously imitating the tone and mannerisms of the male preacher with whom we work when it's our turn to preach, or of adopting the attitudes of male colleagues without developing our own style in appropriate response to our ministries, and according to our relationship with Christ and with one another as women of God. We are more fortunate than our male colleagues in some ways, for it's even easier for men to fall into a pattern laid out for them by some older male colleague. As women, we're probably more conscious of the need to develop our own styles from the onset. The problem lies in the fact that we are less likely to have support in creating our own models than men in similar situations, for we are more likely to find ourselves alone, without affirmation from others sharing a similar process. This is when it becomes necessary to seek out other women, to create our own networks of support and accountability.

As women who are priests, we are sacramental women, persons who focus on the sacramental dimension of life. Our own outward signs need to be in harmony with the inward truth of our relationship with God and the worshipping community, and with the whole human community. Not only am I called to priestly ministry, but the lay person in me needs women priests. Priests need priests, too. I need the ministry of priestly persons who are women, to be an outward symbol to me of the part of divinity that is female, the part in whose image I am made. Seeing a female priest at the altar assures me that I don't have to leave my sexuality at the church door when I come to worship, but that I can worship with my body as well as my heart and soul and mind, wholly joining the Great Dance. One of the beautiful moments of my ministry was early on, when a lay woman told me one Sunday morning that seeing me vested in the sanctuary during the liturgy woke her up to her own full participation in the Church as a daughter of God.

The one thing that women can bring to the priesthood that hasn't been there before is a genuine value for femaleness. Imitating society rather than Christ, the Church has failed to value femaleness. Even the compensatory devotion to Mary has failed to acknowledge the reality of her human sexuality and personality. When value has been restored to femaleness in the Church and in society, when its inherent goodness and integrity are no longer questioned or denied, then it will no longer be necessary for me to make the affirmation of myself as a *woman* priest. I wait for the day when womanhood and manhood will be celebrated equally in the human community, and I will no longer be womanpriest, but *priest.* I do not think that day will come during my lifetime, or in several lifetimes to come, but for this reason all the more, I am committed to its coming.

Meanwhile, in redefining ourselves, we Christian women need to know that we don't have to be martyrs to earn the

171

respect of God—we have to be *heroes.* In the past we've identified with the self-sacrificing Savior, clinging to the cross—Christ's and ours—long after we should have let go of it in recognition of the resurrection—Christ's and ours. Jesus not only died for our sakes, he rose into our life for our sakes, that we could do likewise. It's time for Christian women to climb down off our crosses, to put them aside, to start acting like redeemed people, to begin to live resurrected lives, accepting the fullness and newness of life we are so freely offered. Now, when our dedication is most crucial, when we need to move into the future with courage and conviction and redemptive energy, we need to let go of the unnecessary burdens of our lives, freeing ourselves to carry only those that are necessary.

I was thinking about this one day shortly before the official recognition of my priesthood. It occurred to me that not one of us had lain passively back and allowed herself to be martyred in the difficult times since our ordinations to the priesthood. This is very different behavior from that which most of us were taught: no longer were we suffering sweetly for Jesus—we were claiming the goodness of our own creation and accepting the redemption offered to us in Christ. In a half-serious, half-playful mood, I wrote:

Women, Lay Down Your Crosses, Wear Only Butterflies

> In the old days,
> Perpetua and Felicity
> and their Company,
> the Martyrs of Lyon,
> the Sixteen Carmelites
> of Campagne,
> Virgins of Triest—
> Chicago Seven,
> Cantonville Nine
> and Philadelphia Eleven.

Oh, the days of martyrs,
Yes, the days of saints
and martyrs, glorious,

going out with smells and bells,
up in smoke, blood, guts, crosiers all.

"Alla the Illicit
and Her Companions"
keeping illicit company
with crouching angels,
we poor devils left behind
on the calendar of saints
because we refused
the martyr's crown,
believing truly heaven
is here, the realm
begins within.

The age of dead martyrs
gives way to living heroes.
At last we are learning
to choose *life*, to choose it *all*.

The last stanza speaks not of Episcopal women priests, but of all women rising in fear and courage to the challenge of becoming all we can be in our own small moment in history.

We women, who have been culturally conditioned to be self-effacing, overly modest, and unrealistically sacrificial, are often able to fight for justice for everyone but ourselves. Since we are more than half the human race, it's clear to me that if we fail in justice for ourselves, we fail the human race. I have heard feminism described as "organized selfishiness." I suppose this could equally be said of any human effort to enhance the human condition. In actuality, feminism has deep roots in Christian theology, not only as a movement motivated by

173

justice, but as one motivated by grace—by human and divine gifts.

The Christian basis for the philosophy of feminism is the belief that women and men are created equally in the image of God; the politics of feminism is the actualization, by women and men, of that belief. Many people say, "Why don't you talk about humanism? Why all this emphasis on feminism?" My response to that is humanism, the actualization of our human potentiality, is the general goal for which feminism is the specific means. Since we live in a one-sided culture in favor of maleness, the essential place to restore balance is in the restoration of value to the female side of life. Hence, feminism is the obvious and essential emphasis in correcting the evils of domination in a patriarchal culture. If we lived in an oppressive female-dominated society, I suppose we would be "masculists" at this point in history. We begin with our reality and we move toward our goal, but the specific way cannot be bypassed in order to reach the end we seek. Human liberation is the general abstraction that can only be achieved by specific and concrete liberation movements among women, men, people of color, people of poverty, the young, the aged, and all who can find group identity in common oppression of any kind.

I am not a woman priest because I am a feminist; I am a feminist because I am a woman called to priesthood in a male-oriented institution that refused to celebrate that calling. I became aware of a personal vocation to the priesthood of Christ and of the validity and necessity of the Women's Liberation Movement at the same time. Paul wrote to the Galatians, "When Christ freed us, he meant that we should remain free. Stand firm, therefore, and do not submit again to the yoke of slavery." Yet we have submitted, again and again, and we have reinforced one another's slavery. While slavery presses down (oppresses) our full humanity and thus limits our growth and cuts off our expressive capabilities, it is in many ways easier to

174

bear than the freedom of Christ. Slaves know what is expected of them, and have only to conform. They have no responsibility. Slavery is a very seductive form of security, for it requires little more than filling another's demand for the assurance of being accepted. Such acceptance is, however, a form of death. The challenge to lay claim upon the freedom to create one's own life is infinitely harder by comparison with the most difficult demands of enslavement, as life itself is more difficult than death.

Because I see the choice between life and death laid out in the scriptures as the choice between freedom and spiritual slavery, I choose to align myself with the human forces of liberation in the holy struggle for human dignity. I am a feminist because I am a Christian.

The ministry of a Christian feminist is to be a missionary to the Churches, to challenge them to practice the redemption they preach. Christian feminists confront the Churches with the ecclesiastical slavery of both sexes: men are enslaved to rigid forms of power as women are enslaved to powerlessness. The freedom of Christ exists in genuine mutuality experienced in human relationships, the mutuality that Jesus realized with his friends, the mutuality that exploits no one, reveres the gifts of all.

Women cannot hoard the Christian virtues of humility, self-sacrifice, generosity, and modesty; neither can we reject the Christian virtues of leadership, decisive action, prophecy, strength, and assertion. Genuine mutuality means the free sharing of these traits, so that neither we nor our brothers are confined to a limited experience of the gifts of the Holy Spirit or are cut off from the fullness of life in Christ. Women are also called to be responsible participants and leaders in the Christian community, and men are also called to follow Christ in humility, compassion, and self-sacrifice.

It isn't enough for women to join the men at the altar or conference table; men have to join the women in washing the

175

linens and baking the bread. Likewise, in our larger human communities, the integration of women into executive positions in the professions will do little for human liberation until men are completely free to raise children and be homemakers. Roles do not the person make, so let's be flexible with our roles for each person's sake! Let the unique gifts and skills of everyone be freely expressed in various ways for the good of all.

We Are The Church

One Sunday morning in the middle of winter last year, I went to a nearby parish church for Sunday services, simply as a member of the congregation. My view from the pew was frankly alienating.

I heard from the scriptures that God our Father cares for the needs of men; I heard that we must love our brothers; and I heard that it is a wonderful thing to become a son of God. These words came to us through the male ministers of the community. They stood far away from us, in front of us, and elevated above us on a raised platform that was holy space. There were no women in the holy space. The women were huddled together below, yet cut off from one another lined up in rows, forced to face each other's backs. Our only access to the holy was through the benevolence of the male ruling class in the spiritual community, perfectly illustrating Milton's phrase, "he for God alone, she for God in him."

Week after week women come to these services, submitting like sheep to patriarchal rituals that shut them out in language and imagery, presenting a distorted picture of God and of their place in the sight—or out of the sight—of God. We bow our heads meekly, submissively, acknowledging our unworthiness and forgetting our femaleness, which we have graciously left at home lest it contaminate this temple of

God. We kneel before a sometimes generous, sometimes judging male God, and we hear a male priest speak of this God's love for men and angels. All our lives we have somehow been able to develop a spirituality for ourselves despite these obstacles, learning long ago how to do the mental gymnastics necessary to translate what we see and hear so that it somehow includes us. Unfortunately, we have also tried to translate ourselves, thus doing violence to our true Godlike natures in order to fit them into the images portrayed for us.

And then people ask, "Why do these women want to be men?" In the Creed we say that Christ died for us men and for our salvation; in the Gloria we pray for peace and goodwill toward men; we hear that man is created in God's own image; we pray for all mankind, work toward the brotherhood of man,[1] and learn of the infinite blessedness of the sons of God. What woman on earth wouldn't want to be part of these good things? "Well, of course all these phrases mean women too," comes the response. Rightly speaking, generic language is only valid if what is true of the whole is equally true of the parts: a rose is truly both a rose and a flower; a samoyed in truly both a samoyed and a dog. A woman, however, cannot be described as both *a woman* and *a man,* for man *also* means the *opposite* of woman (as, Is your teacher a man *or* a woman?). Originally in our language, the words for woman and man were *wif* and *wer,* and the word *man* really did mean *human.* But the word *man* was linguistically appropriated to mean adult male human, as well as human, thus identifying humanness with maleness. Femaleness then became, by a linguistic quirk, *other* than human. Since language both reflects and reinforces attitudes, we need to be sensitive to the way in which our use of language is dehumanizing to

---

[1] The Archbishop of Canterbury in a public message in 1977 directed Episcopalians to "love the brethren." As my grandmother would have said, "What about the 'sisteren'?"

women, and we need to *change* our use of language, in fact, re-authenticate it. If the language really *did* include us, then there would be nothing wrong with referring to my mother as *he*, my sister as *the man* sitting in the green chair, or myself as my parents' *son*, or a *son of God*. Likewise, there would be nothing wrong with speaking of the sisterhood of womankind and claiming that it included both sexes. The generic problem, besides its being linguistically and philosophically inauthentic, is that the language can be used against women whenever it suits the (male-ruled) system to do so.[2] In the formation of American values, our founding fathers' phrase, "all men are created equal," in fact meant all white middle class males are created equal, a point not missed by Abigail Adams when she counseled her spouse to "remember the ladies." (If it were not so, we would have no need of the Emancipation Proclamation, the Civil Rights Act of 1964, or the Equal Rights Amendment in the 1970's.)

The psychological pain that attitudes convey in language can be great to a woman, no less so when the attitudes are unconscious or the language is used thoughtlessly. When I go to church and hear how completely I am excluded as a woman, the female side of me cries out to be recognized and loved. I leave such services feeling lost and lonely, cut off from my God, my sisters and brothers, my self. I can no longer make meaning out of this for myself, having seen it for what it is: an unconscionable betrayal of truth through unthinking carelessness and neglect of the symbols we use. The symbols are important, vital links of communication, or we wouldn't use them. When they communicate falsehood and

---

[2] A diocesan newspaper this month asked "What can you do for your hungry brothers?" Demographers' reports show that among starving peoples, it is girl-children and nursing mothers who are allowed to die first; food will be given to the infant son, and the infant daughter will be sacrificed. Hunger on all levels affects females—usually first.

179

evil, they become demonic. They diminish human spirituality and humanhood itself. Going to church breaks my heart, because there are no images there to tell me God knows and cares that I'm alive as a woman. And it's *as a woman* that I am *human*.

The dilemma shared by women in the Episcopal Church has been in the double message we've heard all our lives, when our Fathers in God told us that we're truly sons of God, but that we can't be priests, spiritual leaders, or decision-makers because we're not men. Kept confused, we were excluded from full participation in the Episcopal Church, a men's club that is 58% female.[3]

There is something demonic in all of this. The demonic is anything that has power to isolate us—from God, from one another, from ourselves. While listening to a sermon delivered by a colleague of mine, suddenly I realized that what he was saying about Jesus's encounter with the demonic legion in the gospel related to my own relationship with the Church. Church is where I come seeking inclusion and find exclusion, seeking wholeness and find fragmentation, seeking forgiveness and affirmation and find accusation and denial. The Church is my demon. In his sermon, my colleague put forth the question, "What do we do with our demons?" Jesus's response to the demonic was to get closer to it, to identify it, to be recognized by it, finally to match powers with it.

How can I relate to the Church my demon? If I run from it, it will follow me, for I will find it inside me wherever I go. Our demons exist inside us along with divine grace. Perhaps, if I tried to leave my demon, I would also be abandoning indwelling grace, abandoning my *self*. Knowing this has kept me very clear on knowing that I couldn't just leave the

---

[3] *Religion in America,* 1976, Gallup Opinion Index.

180

Church, since it has shaped much of who I am. I'd be haunted forever by its ghost in my soul. The only thing to do is to stand firm and face it. Yet, I can't do this alone. I must be free to ask for as well as offer help in dealing with alienation, grief, anger, frustration, despair, hope.

The phrase applied to the Episcopal Church's definition of mission, "mutual responsibility and interdependence," describes a genuine way of meeting our demons together by creating community. The Church, paradoxically, is the place of my demons, and the place I come to share my demons. The shape of my yearning turns me toward others who also bravely face their demons in the company of Christ.

The Christian community calls us out of isolation and into a common vision of justice, freedom, and loving community, where each person can find a place in the whole. Christian community is one created not only out of need, but out of overflow, for when people are genuinely engaged with their demons, at some point we come to recognize the angel of God; transformation takes place, and our need becomes fullness, abundance. Then others can catch the overflowing power and energy of renewed love, without which no community can sustain itself. The alternative is waste, diminishment through withdrawal leading to privatism, panic, and a kind of death.

Being isolated means being trapped, cornered off from the freedom of the community, of experiencing oneself through interaction with others. It means being closed off from the other side. It's like being caught in a fire. My priest friend who preached on demons drew this comparison, recalling a newspaper story about a fire in a New York City apartment building. Everyone had escaped except for a young girl named Maria. Smoke in the burning building was so thick that Maria could see nothing at all. She had no idea how to escape. Her father was on the street below. He called out to her over and over, "Maria! Maria!" She heard her name and she managed to move steadily toward the window from which the sound came. Then her father said, "Maria, jump! I have my arms stretched out for you." She jumped and was saved.

When we can't get sight of God, when we hardly know where or who we are, when we fail to see that someone is there with arms outstretched to us, our only chance is to leap in faith, trusting that there is love on the other side.

We fear our demons because we don't know where they will take us. We can't be certain of being caught by loving arms more than by the fire around us. But the pull toward life is strong. Sometimes our demons drive us toward more life, if we can find the courage to jump into the unknown, into mystery, into love.

It's all right to have demons. We all do. We all have things that bind us, compel us, confine us, diminish us. But sharing our demons saves us somehow. The community of faith holds us in a common vision that recognizes the yearning in us toward life, toward integrity of being, toward rhythms of solitude and togetherness. Theology and morality become fused as the community makes appropriate collective (political) responses to the concrete situations of the human condition in its own name, and transcending itself, in the name of Christ.

The exercising of moral courage is a political act: it involves others besides ourselves. Political interaction in the human community and in the Christian community is corporate response to life situations; at its best it is the moral manifestation of a vision in action. I see all of history as a great field of human creation in which vision becomes action in a continuous, simultaneous process. Personal and corporate history are formed out of the creative development of perception, experience, and personality (what we've expressly made of ourselves). On the personal level, history is the unfolding of vocation, discovered in the meaning that

182

one's life takes on in exploring a particular direction or possibility.

To experience a vocation—which everyone does in a unique way—is to acknowledge the total gift of life to us, where our past experience and personal gifts have brought us, what our life has come to. This recognition of meaning is in itself a "coming-to," an awakening in our perception and understanding of relationships and experiences that have informed the person we've become. Experiencing a vocation is a kind of advent experience. We *come-to,* and in coming-to we become ready to respond to God and the world as they come to meet us. A vocation, then, is the integration of self-perception and world-perception in relationship to God. To be authentic, it must be *both* experienced within oneself and affirmed by a community.

We don't have to figure out God's fixed blueprint for our lives. We have to create our own blueprint as we go. God isn't the great puppeteer in the sky who pulls our strings to see us jump and fall, leaving us desperately trying to figure out what comes next, or what we're supposed to be doing with our lives. God's will for us isn't a series of specifics that we have to be clever enough to guess. God's will for us is that we become whole by whatever means are available, and by the choices we make. Our task is to act as conscious agents of our own lives, creatively discovering what makes us whole at this moment, at this place. When we're on the right track, we know because we feel healthy and alive. This is how I experience vocation. Others would describe it differently, whether their vocation is to philosophy, science, education, manual work, politics, child-raising, or the development of human life through interaction with others in a thousand ways, each like no other way in the world. Vocation is the interaction of one's needs, gifts, skills, conscious and unconscious desires, past and present, *psyche* and *soma,* intentions and actions, possibilities and powers, heredity and environment, time and space, nature and grace. It's the direction one's life takes from within, manifested, as Teilhard would say, by an inner excess of tension moving outward.

As vocation is the hearing, vision is the seeing of the meaning of one's own mystery, of the total pattern of one's own life in relation to the whole of human community, and in relation to God. Vision is the inner organization necessary for action. A vision is the creative shape of a person's calling.

Vision became action for me when I responded to the calling toward priesthood by going to Philadelphia. I heard, from deep within, a calling that drew me along this particular path of possibility. I saw the way in which to respond, and this became my vision, which frightened me and gave me the confidence and courage to act at the same time. Vision is always limited, determined by future events and unknown responses from others. Sometimes we are only half-conscious of the mystery into which we are being drawn, and that's when it's necessary to act on faith, trusting our own processes even when they are only partially apparent to us. As soon as I begin to see, things change. My perception is constantly having to adjust and catch up with the unfolding reality and its meaning. My eyes may never be fully open until the hour of my death, when the process will change so radically that it will appear to be over.

I believe that there is always a connection between personal vocation and collective or corporate vision. Each person in the prophetic community has something to contribute. The Christian community is enriched and sustained by its members who are also connected with movements for justice beyond it. I believe that when the Church cannot speak to the world for God, God can speak to the Church through the world. The Church is in the world, and the world is in the Church, and God uses all available means to speak to all of us at any moment in history. I see the Women's Liberation Movement and the various other liberation movements as

184

inspired by the Holy Spirit, and judged like every movement of the Spirit, by the results they bear—by their fruits. Nature and grace are not antitheses, for we were born into Original Grace before original sin was invented, and the incarnation has proven that God holds dear everything that is human, making no false separations between matter and spirit, secular and sacred, but using all created things as a way of loving access to us, no matter how ambitiously we try to block out that possibility.

The whole Church is constantly living out the paschal[4] mystery of Christ, dying and being reborn, resurrecting from the burning fires of the Spirit, emerging from its own ashes in a perennial phoenix dance. The prophetic community retains its integrity by affirming life through an ongoing willingness to die to its old self. The liberation process involves constantly dying to the old securities. Security is sometimes the price of moral integrity, and embracing insecurity for the sake of something larger and truer than before is, like birth, both terrifying and exhilarating. Finding ourselves always in transition, at times more dramatically than others, we approach our own transformation with mixed feelings of grief and resistance, joy and eagerness. New intrudes upon old, and as they inelegantly overlap through times of transition, we experience the hard labor of a people giving birth to ourselves.

Through the terror of transformation, we come to know individually and corporately the explosive joy of being fully alive. In being faithful to the many little deaths of letting go of the past, we enter the present in one another's presence with faithfulness and trust. This is the nature of the continuous process of renewal. The death and rebirth in it become the primary mystery and fact of nature and of history. Christ

---

[4] The Passover theme of death and deliverance, loss and renewal, sacrifice and new life.

showed forth this mystery in his life, not only in the drama of Calvary and the empty tomb, but also through the daily encounters with people at Bethany, in Jerusalem, Nazareth, and on the road, in the desolation of the crowds as well as in deepest solitude with God.

The Church as a prophetic community needs continuously to be open to self-evaluation. To clearly hear and speak the purposes of God among us we need to search our corporate soul for signs of moral integrity and health, or signs of disintegration. The quest for ethical wisdom is the moral dimension of our life together. This quest involves the asking of questions that can help us to penetrate and perceive our own interaction.

I have been living with three questions concerning the Church, seeking through them deeper understanding of my own relationship to and in the Christian community, inside the institution and beyond.

My first question is, "Who is the Church?"

Is it the male hierarchy? The integrated laity? The patriarchal socio-religious ruling class that excluded women from its ministry and values? Is it divinely inspired, often invisible saints? Corrupt sinners? These possibilities suggest the underlying question, "What is the Church?" Is the Church outside ourselves or within us? Is it a human community or a divine institution? Is it a bond of faith or a power system? Is it combinations of some or many or all of these? Sometimes, when I give myself an answer to the question, "Who is the Church," I hear myself speaking in dichotomies. When I'm feeling particularly excluded as a woman by the male-run power structure, I feel that "they" define the Church as themselves and "us" (women) as *other*. When I'm feeling responsible and confident and generally positive about my participation in the Christian community, I define the Church as "we." In these moments, which I feel represent the ideal for which many of us strive, I perceive the Church as all of us together, bonded by faith in God through Christ and the

186

Holy Spirit at work in the world. I see us, in these moments that seem particularly clear, as co-responsible participants in a self-determining and Spirit-centered community.

My second question is, "For whom is the Church?"

Is it for the rich, the middle class, the elect, according to the capitalistic code of material success? Is it for the priest caste? Is it for married heterosexual prosperous males who apply machismo ethics to the conquest of pagan (non-conformist) cultures in the name of Christianity? Or is the Church for everyone, without exception, without exclusion, without condition?

My third question is, "How is the Church what it is?"

Is it through the acquisition of wealth and power? Through real estate and other property? Through patterning itself (rather badly) after complex business corporations? Through buying stock in the military-industrial machine? Through shepherding the faithful into geographical corrals? Through statistical games (how many people this year did we baptize, bury, communicate, marry, confirm, convert, feed, clothe, or shelter)? Or is it through altogether other means? Is it through human interactions motivated by passion for justice and freedom and love that was in Christ?

An Open Conference on the Ministry of Women meeting in St. Louis early in 1977 includes among its women-oriented workshops one called "Responsible Living." Responsible living begins with the courage to take on simple existential questions such as those I've posed, and living them out in the context of a concerned community.

As women in the Church, responsible living involves our corporate affirmation that *we are the Church*. We are not "other." We are joint heirs of salvation—of whole-making—with our brothers in Christ. We, too, are responsible for the integrity of the organism called the Body of Christ.

Living our responsibility for the Body of Christ requires our participation in it at all levels, including levels of spiritual

187

and administrative leadership. Ordination for women is important as the actualization of female freedom and responsibility in the Church, and as a symbol to all women of their participation in the Church's leadership and sacramental life. Today I received a letter from a Roman Catholic friend, in which she described to me her growing sense of calling to the priesthood. She shared with me her frustrations in ministering to people, especially to women during pregnancy and childbirth, and not being able to follow through sacramentally in moments of deepest meaning, such as Baptism, Eucharist, and the Sacrament of Reconciliation. She leads a Theology for Mothers group, and is sensitive to the fact that each time she has to call in a priest from outside to preside at the Eucharist, the integrity of each woman present is violated, for the Church hierarchy says to them that their own priesthood as women is invalid when they experience it to be genuinely filled with meaning, power, and truth. My friend told me that when she was a child she informed her mother that she wanted to be a priest. Her mother's response was representative of the institutional Church's: "Little girls can't be priests." Her answer was not only logical but theological: "I don't want to be a priest when I'm a little girl, I want to be a priest when I'm grown up." Two weeks ago my friend had a dream: "I was trying to climb out of a cloistered garden over a church roof because I couldn't go through the door since I didn't have the key. It was terribly hard work, but worth it because I had to get to the other side. Then I was walking in the door from the street side with a parish council-type group behind me, holding a key in my hand and laughing and saying to them 'see—it's so easy when you have the key,' and I woke up *knowing* (that's the only word I have for it) that ordination was the *key* to the kind of work that I want to be doing." Later in her letter, my friend says, "I find that I'm getting more and more radical, and there's nothing wrong with that if it leads to growth, but I'm afraid of the bitterness that comes sometimes when I can't move forward

188

simply because I'm a woman. The frustration gets so intense when I think it's something that I should be doing and will probably have to answer for someday for not doing. It is deeply burned in my brain that the only servant who was condemned was the one who buried his/her talent because of fear, so at least I have to try. . . . "

The inclusion of women into the institutional hierarchy will have no effect on the Christian community unless the hierarchy is radically transformed by it. Victory over sexism has by no means been won because women now have access to the priesthood. Access to priesthood is not success over sexism, but only the brink of another long phase in the task of the Church's social mission to destroy its own structural evils of domination and oppression. The battered souls of women represent a demoralized spiritual structure. They and it can only be healed if we take action now, recognizing that this is not the moment of triumph, but of deepest challenge. The most critical times usually occur when we are most weary of the struggle, most likely to fall back into false security. Then all is lost, and life is worse than before, for then we become guilty of betraying ourselves through fatigue and fear.

Christian feminists are Christian revolutionaries: we want to *turn the Church back* to its original health and oneness in Christ. We are revolutionaries in another sense, in that we can't stand injustice. The revolutionary vision perceives the basic organic connection and interrelationship of everything in the universe. The Christian revolutionary recognizes the incarnational interdependence among all living creatures, for we have all been loved into being by one Creator. The need underlying the revolutionary vision is the yearning toward oneness with those beings from whom we have been alienated by the denial of community, freedom, and justice. Our unquenchable grief is in a longing for those faces through whom we can no longer see the clarifying and integrating love of the Creator. Alienation has covered the created forms and made community a distant dream. Disintegration—dis-integrity—sets in. The Christian revolutionary cannot bear the harm done to God's creatures by this alienation of injustice, and proceeds to rage against it. The revolutionary thus reaches out to lay claim on the promise of salvation, of wholeness, pointing to the heart of our moral life together.

Morality in the Christian community flows spontaneously out of a shared perception of Christ's love. It is a shared attitude of desire for the common good, an attitude of well-wishing toward life so forceful that it shapes the good it intends. Genuine morality is the actualized overflow of the love of Christ into the world; it is an acted yearning for the wholeness and well-being of others. It is, finally, a mutual empowerment toward wholeness in creation.

When the power of the Holy Spirit is present among us, we come in touch with our own power to create a world of values. Our power becomes informed with the consciousness of Christ, so that we can act "in one mind with Christ." We remain free to accept and use the gifts of the Holy Spirit in the building of a truly charismatic community, a community of cooperation in which functions are determined by need and gifts or skills, and leadership is both shared and entrusted by the whole to some in whom leadership emerges as a grace. Rigid structures that identify value with vertical position or function are replaced by flexible structures where the gifts of all are equally valued. As people work together to transform oppressive power structures into liberating communities, exploitative power is replaced by the integrative power that enables us to assert that we are children of God, and to claim the Church as our responsibility. In a gradually shared leadership, mutual service expresses mutual concern. In responding appropriately and openly to the needs of the world and of each other, the gifts of all can be realized. Acknowledging our

190

mistakes and our consistent ability to wound one another, we can learn to forgive and encourage each other through the process.

Through a commitment to self-evaluation, we can discern whether or not our authority comes from Christ, whether or not we are of one mind with Christ. We can claim the values of personal liberty and responsibility exemplified by Christ, making our liturgies and our laws more Christ-like and more humane in language, imagery, and definition, purifying our self-concept through corporate questioning, replacing artificiality with genuineness, separation with communion, and values of law as an end with values of humanity and generosity.

I see the renewing Christian community as the body that shows forth the mind of Christ in the Church and in the world today. We have been given the gratuitous gifts of reconciliation, freedom, forgiveness, justice, and peace, in order to express the mind of Christ to those we serve with authenticity. When each generation of Christians accepts the Spirit's challenge and takes on the laborious task of re-visioning the Church, faith can remain a living thing, a source of power and meaning for those who share it. But when a generation unthinkingly tries to assimilate what has been passed down to it from the past without creating its own vision and response, faith becomes a dead weight, an object, a burden. The only energy then is in the strained effort to preserve this heavy thing, this dead weight of tradition that has ceased to grow, that has become an end in itself and is no longer a means toward fullness in Christ.

This refusal to grow is a corruption of tradition, as exploitation is a corruption of authority. The Latin *traditio* was a physical hand-to-hand surrender from one person to another, and it necessitated physical change. Tradition has been taken by some to mean changelessness, when in fact, change is the essence of tradition. Nothing can be passed on

191

from one person to another without being changed in the process, for each new generation's response effects a new way of existing for whatever comes down to us from the past.

When the Church fails in its call to become a prophetic, charismatic, caring, concerned, and cooperative community, representatives may be called up out of the community to assume the task of judgment and encouragement for the whole. These are the loyal rebels, the prophets who speak to the Church when the Church can no longer speak to itself or to the world. Prophets speak with the authority of holiness, striving to re-call the community of faith to its own authority of holiness through the gifts which have been dispensed freely and without discrimination throughout it.

The holy rebel is loyal to the community while challenging the systemic evil within it. If the community's response is positive, charisms can once again emerge through restored relationships of mutual love and respect. The loyal rebel works with what appears to be a furious desperation to bring this about, knowing that if the Church doesn't turn away from death, gifts will go wasted, integrity will be forfeited, the community will disintegrate.

The loyal rebels are the chancers and changers who are consumed with a vision toward change aimed at the enhancement of life. Their role is priestly; they experience sacrifice. They offer themselves as catalysts, trying to recall the pilgrim Church to its original quest for truth. Their presence can have an effect on the Church that is simultaneously freeing and annoying. Loyal rebels are given to speaking their own truth within the community, challenging others to do likewise, until the authentic word is restored to the whole, and people can once again speak the truth to God and each other.

Prophets and rebels are as leary of overmuch praise as they are weary of unpopularity. Made into victory symbols or villains inappropriately and often deprived of privacy, they are simply trying to do a job that needs to be done. They don't want acclamation so much as the affirmation of camaraderie in the task. They don't want to be hoisted on people's shoulders, but to walk shoulder to shoulder through the long marches for justice and truth.

When my own life and the lives of other women in the Church have touched on the prophetic function of the Church, we have experienced fatigue and rejection and sometimes physical abuse. We have been treated like angels or devils. (I was once called a devil by an audience participant during a panel discussion, and a sister priest of mine was once scratched so badly by a young male priest at the altar rail after he took communion from her that she had to have stitches.) Frequently we have been denied human decencies, either through too much deference or too much resentment because people have objectified us one way or the other. This is probably due to the frightening power of some of the things we say and do, which present a threat to security for many people. I know that tremendous courage is needed to stick with the process. Many times I have wanted to disclaim my responsibility for the Church. I have wanted to run away. What has kept me going has been the knowledge that the task is not mine, but ours and that there can be genuine joy in the sharing.

The main point is that we need each other. No one can change the world by herself. In fact, survival, that most basic factor, depends on staying in touch with others who can heal us when we have forgotten how to heal ourselves. About midway through my three years of ecclesial limbo I began to realize some of these things—about survival, community, healing, the need for us as women to take turns supporting and being supported by one another, to stagger our energies so that we don't all burn out at the same time and lose what we have gained. I wrote down some of the things I learned about the tensions between the personal and the political and how to deal with them while confronting the Church with the Gospel against difficult odds.

Some definitions for psychic survival:

Alien Territory:	Unfriendly psychic space; people who disagree with/disapprove of who you are; vibrations hostile to your basic sense of self. Recognize it.
Creativity:	Self-healing, self-renewal. Pouring yourself into something you make outside yourself, and coming out of it fresh. Be creative in a thousand ways. *Everything is connected.*
Escape Hatch:	Someone to take with you when you have to enter alien territory for missionary or other purposes. A friendly psychic space someone creates for you by on the spot support. Never be without one.
Extreme Fantasy:	In really tight necessary spots, a fantasy of what you would be doing now instead of what you are doing if you only had the (a) guts, (b) time, (c) money; extreme because this fantasy is truly fantastic to make up for the real mess you're in, and to keep you from doing anything silly such as trying to run away to fulfill your fantasies.

194

	Keep one on the back burner. . . . Who knows?
Fantasy:	Same as above only ongoing and more feasible.
	Remember the art of *possibility!*
Humor/Laughter:	Laughter is a holy gift, like tears, used appropriately. As tears are the baptism of the soul, laughter is smiling wisdom.
	Make it your best tool.
Safety Zone:	Friendly psychic space; people who affirm who you are and allow you to discover whom you can become. Someone at the other end of a telephone should you find yourself (God forbid!) returning from alien territory without your escape hatch.
	Always have access to it.
Screaming Sessions:	Just what it sounds like. Especially good in a moving car with the windows rolled up, or alone with a tether ball or punching bag. Be sure to keep your throat wide open, and let the sound come up from your feet.
	Use frequently, as needed.
Survival:	Especially in dealing with institutions, knowing that you can play their games and still keep your in-

195

	tegrity. Sometimes involves compromise, sometimes subversion.
	It works, surprisingly.
Self-love:	Out of order because most important. Being able to look in the mirror and say, "You are a child of God. You're not such a bad person. I like you." Being able to name things about yourself that you love.
	Know that you are an image of God.

Each generation of Christians has to face Christ as if for the first time, and learn from Jesus the authority of a teaching and healing that have redemptive power in the world. Jesus, the Word of God, spoke himself into a world that needed the power of personal authority and not the defenses of rigid laws or spiritless observances. The Word became flesh in the form of our humanity in order to speak to us with a human voice that we could recognize and obey (*hear deeply*) with love.

That is the challenge as I see it, the challenge we take on when we realize that the Church is not a separate entity, it is us. We are right to be frightened by the huge responsibility of this claim, but we are also right in taking courage from one another. We are all holding each other up all the time.

Today in the Churches, many holy women have been given a prophetic task and a moral vision for the health of the whole Church. These persons have sometimes acted as loyal rebels, to call the Church back to the mind of Christ. They do this so the Church may become a new people that can once again speak prophetic words of peace, power, light, and hope to the world.

In summary, I quote the Episcopal Church Bulletin for the Fourth Sunday in Epiphany in 1976:

It is the prophetic function ... to examine the implications of the faith in our daily lives. This needs to be done lovingly and humbly, yet fearlessly, recognizing that all are judged, including the prophet, just as all are loved.

And I give you my own response to Galatians 5:1:[1]

Freedom

Freedom is death,
being Absolute Possibility,
unbearable waiting
for the escape
into a new cage
where
freedom as death will
return, reclaim us,
until we escape
into a new cage
until
freedom as life
lights us
and we can
rise,
wounded but healed
from our comforting chains.

---

[1] "When Christ freed us he meant us to remain free. Stand firm, therefore, and do not submit again to the yoke of slavery." (Jerusalem Bible)

God Is A Verb

God
is
a
verb.

God is One
mighty
roaring
verb.

God is
One

God is
mighty

God is
roaring

God
Is
a verb
roaring

God-Is.

This verb named God
we now name New
Being,
solar/lunar/sidereal
MOTION
soaring
breathing   burning   lightning
ultrasonic
SOUND.

God is
in me
I know, being
new,
stretch   strike   light-
ning,
soar-sound.
Godlike

sometimes I just have to
rise up and *R O A R*

    In my dream, I have just received a check in the mail for
a book that I've published. Since I have no recollection of
having written a book, let alone having published it, I decide
to go out and buy a copy to find out what I've said. I go to the
grocery store and take my cart to the book section that is
between fruit and milk. I recognize my book instantly: it's a
glossy black soft-covered book with only the word SPIRIT in
glossy white on the cover. I pick it up and open it to find my
name on the inside. Instead of my actual name, the name
Alice Rice is in the upper right-hand corner of the inside leaf.
I accept this pseudonym and am pleased. When I awaken and

amplify the dream with conscious associations, I realize that Alice is the name of a physician whom I greatly admire, and Rice is the last name of a nurse I knew as a child. I discover the etymology of the names: Alice from Greek *alethea, truth;* and rice from Sanskrit *rizon, seed.* Associations evoked by the dream's images are light out of darkness, the seed of truth hidden within, healing women, and nourishment, in the context of a personal spirituality that is shared with others in a public but private way through symbolic anonymity. The life of the Spirit is available in the grocery store with other food in the most natural way; there is a price on it—it's something of value, and must be taken and used to be purposeful.

The ecstatic and the mundane exist together unself-consciously.

Dreams have always impressed me as spontaneous works of art, produced by the unconscious parts of the psyche with breathtaking clarity. I begin sharing with you my thoughts on spirituality by describing one of my own dreams because I believe that authentic spirituality is personal, spontaneous, and clearly expressed, though not always fully conscious. Our dreams are a valid expression of spirituality, for they tell of the life of the soul, as do our waking fantasies, images, and collective myths.

If theology is the rational attempt to describe God and our relationship with the holy, spirituality is the pararational, existential living-out of our God-experience and our relationship with the holy.

Today more than ever before in the history of spiritual consciousness, we have an opportunity to express our personal and collective spiritual life holistically. The life of the spirit is not separate from the whole of human life. The spirit is alive through the passions of the body and of the mind, and it expresses itself in living relationships with other beings, seen and unseen.

The language of the spirit is symbol, for symbolism in

the psychological sense is simply the means we make for expressing the unexpressible. Symbols are charged by the aura of mystery in what they express and must leave unexpressed, but clearly felt. Mystery is the part of life that defies definition. It isn't something that can be solved, for by its very nature, it constitutes a limitless power to exist beyond merely rational comprehension. Mystery is the part of life that can't be captured, but which tends to capture us. As Gabriel Marcel wrote, mystery isn't a problem to be solved, but a reality to be lived. Mystery is the living part of speech beyond language, of hearing beyond sound, of vision beyond sight. Mystery is where theology ends and spirituality begins. It is the threshold at which reason surrenders to the knowing capacity of the whole organism. Theologians have always recognized the purpose of their work to be preparatory to the activity of the spirit, though occasionally the definitive language of theology has intruded upon the experience of the holy, for theology speaks and provides the context of the intellect to a process that also includes the silences of the spirit. The true theologian knows when to speak and describe experience, and when simply to experience. The challenge facing us today is to develop a valid, holistic theology—one that recognizes the female as well as the male aspect of God, and the transcendent as well as the immanent nature of divinity. Reauthenticating our conceptual process is the other side of reauthenticating our worship experience. Both involve expanding images and the creation of accurate language to express our present (certainly, still limited) understanding of God and our relationship to the holy. The contribution of women and our perceptions as females is absolutely essential to this process. As a community of theologians, the Church is called, in each generation, to rebuild its house, to purify its theological structure with a perception that is always new. Now our challenge is to hear the call of the Holy Spirit to make this old house new, to make these walls sing. Then we

201

shall be those whom God calls Rebuilders of Old Houses, and all our walls will shine like sun, no longer grey, but alive with color. The materials we have to use are within ourselves; the structure we have to restore is the one that our forebears in the faith have left to us for an inheritance.

Our approach to the task should be open, generous, honest, and creative. Above all, we should realize that the task is so great that we need to bring to it all that we have, holding back none of the materials of our dreams, myths, revelations, or longings, discriminating and choosing from among these materials those that are appropriate to our collective self-expression in faith and worship.

We need to begin by recognizing the validity and value of our own experience for the corporate good. Contrary to the distorted view of theology often communicated by our teachers in the past, our own experience is relevant to the theology of the whole community. If our theological understanding has no connection with lived experience, it has no validation of its own, and becomes part of the dead weight that burdens us instead of the meaningful context that illumines our lives.

Many things that in the past have been conceptually isolated by theological language are integrated in actual experience. As modern physics now takes account of the interconnection rather than the illegitimate separation of such dynamics as space and time, matter and motion, contemporary theology begins to acknowledge that body and soul, spirit and matter, nature and grace are not rigid dichotomies that need to be reconciled; they are beautifully interacting forces that are experienced and perceived as one. The sensual and spiritual are the same energy playing at different speeds, like poetry and the dance. The last heresy to be refuted by the Church is what I call split-level theology, a framework that sets in opposition things that are intrinsically one, though they can express themselves at either extremity, which we perceive as polarities.

202

The spiritual harm that split-level theology engenders is enormous. While the central fact of the Incarnation is the Christian statement for all time on the goodness of creation, our lives are still contaminated by the ancient Persian myth of the evil of the material world, and the Platonic myth of the need to dematerialize the created world so that it can become again the ideal from which it came. Many Christian ascetics and Neoplatonic philosophers have been misled down the soul-splitting paths of dualism, much to their and our harm. They failed to acknowledge that the incarnational forms of the created world are spirit-charged and do not need further translation or idealization to be holy.

Conceptualization into polarities is useful as a way of recognizing the intrinsic unity of things that appear contradictory, such as light and dark, motion and rest, for each is perceived as an aspect of the other. The problem is that thinkers haven't stopped with individual polarities, but have built whole architectural systems based on expanded categories, and these systems have acquired values. Here is what an expanded split-level philosophical structure looks like, reduced to two columns containing parallel dichotomies:

Column A	Column B
God	Void
Good	Evil
Angel	Devil
Above	Below
Adam	Eve
Male	Female
Yang	Yin
Soul	Body
Spiritual	Sensual
Light	Dark
Life	Death

Energy	Inertia
Creation	Destruction
Intellect	Emotion
Reason	Intuition
Motion	Stillness
Strength	Weakness
Generative	Receptive
Active	Passive
Order	Chaos

What follows is that generally speaking the list in Column A is valued as positive, and the list in Column B is merely the negative aspect of A. This way of thinking contaminates conscious and unconscious attitudes and is psychologically intrinsic to the problems of sexism and racism. When human beings are objectified to fit the plus or minus side of the structure, the basic premise of opposition is dehumanizing and counterproductive. Aspects are inconsistently applied, for, though the system is rigid, some of the oppositions are exchangable. Female, for instance, is sometimes categorized with devil, sometimes with angel; sometimes with sensual, sometimes with spiritual. In either case the result is dehumanizing, for the free flow of energies and mingling aspects is denied.[1]

By breaking up the dichotomies and destroying the split-level system, value can be restored to many things formerly rejected as categorically bad. A theological model for split-level and holistic concepts can be found in doctrines of

---

[1] Reading in a recent book on psychotherapy, I came upon this parenthetical comment illustrating the immediacy of the split-level method and its attitudinal influence on applied sexism: "One does not have the impression, in Freud, that women have a complete human nature—but to be sure, they are therefore somewhat divine."

the Eucharist. The split-level formula for Holy Communion is that bread and wine—base matter—become changed into the sacred forms of body and blood. Matter undergoes substantial destruction to appear in a form more acceptable to God and more edifying to souls. The holistic understanding of Holy Communion is expressed in the doctrine of consubstantiation. Unlike split-level transubstantiation, consubstantiation says that body and blood exist with, not against bread and wine. The grace of Christ's Eucharistic presence doesn't destroy or replace the material substance of the physical elements, but it exists with and through and in them, naturally and super-naturally.

I propose that a theology of consubstantiation be applied to all of life. Everything in the universe is consubstantial with everything else, but in infinite variety of relationships, not at all in the rigid structures such as suggested by the two-column approach. The concept of consubstantiation is one of enhancement, not replacement. Value is determined by the way in which relationships form, not in the things themselves. The holiness of the body may be experienced as an enhancement of the holiness of the mind or spirit, and the creativity of chaos may be seen as the matrix of order. We live in a society that values product over process, but a holistic approach views the two as one. As the medium *is* the message, the process *is* the product, a value to be loved for its own sake. Artists and the best scientists know this functionally and theoretically. I have long cherished the creative process for its own sake, perceiving the creative link between order and chaos, and recently between art and religion on the one hand, and science on the other.

My tendency is to confuse these dynamics rather than to isolate them. In my own life I experience the same reverence for truth and beauty in both the artistic process and priestly ministry. A friend once told me that when she mentioned me

205

to someone else, the response was, "Oh, that Sister Alla. Her only response to life is poetry." Another friend, a colleague in the academic field of speech and drama, told me that during one of my public lectures on the performing arts, someone in the audience whispered to him, "She never stops talking about religion, does she?"[2] It is true that I find breathtaking unities on many levels of experience as I grow more deeply into them. I am coming to understand experientially the meaning of "everything that rises must converge."

While I have been moved by the experience in my own vocation of artist-as-priest, priest-as-artist (or poet-as-priest, priest-as-poet), only recently has the area of science and intellectual speculation occurred to me as a source of experiential unity. This is due almost entirely to Fritjof Capra's beautiful book, *The Tao of Physics,* in which a modern physicist (Capra) comes to a clearer understanding of physics through a close study of Eastern religions. The book moves like a poem. When I read it this fall, I recalled the first words of my geology professor on the opening day of classes at Northwestern University: "In the beginning was the Word, and the Word was . . . hydrogen." Though some professional theologians may find the scientist's attention-grabbing statement to be offensive, those who heard him say it can testify to his reverence. As a scientist, he lives with mystery as priests and poets do, but from a different view. The great interest in astronomy among Christians this Christmas, along with Capra's book, and the memory of my geology professor's open-

---

[2] I *did mention* that the most important thing for a performer is *belief* in the life of the literary text, that the performer's responsibility is, through humbly encountering, yielding and giving to the text, to embody it, show it forth in an *incarnation* that can be perceived by others, and bring others into *communion* with itself!

206

ing statement, caused me to write about chaos and Christmas
from a new perspective this year:

Creation

In the beginning was
hydrogen.
And then
the Explosion.

We, the fragments,
tumbling to Infinity,
part of the One,
expanding the Origins,
starchildren
born out of the Chaos of God.

Incarnation

In the beginning still
was the Word,
spoken into form,
being-become-motion
slow enough for us
to see and touch and hear,
bodying forth a divine love
in human glory
(God-like-Us, We-like-God),
the One, the Very,
became born
into our Chaos,
making it surely
holy for ever.

Mary Daly's fresh theological insight that God, like love, is a verb, gives me tremendous excitement and a sense of expansion, the temple of God at my center opening out like a morning rose. It puts me in touch with God within and God beyond; God active as fire, wind, and water inside me and beyond the universe. My own creativity becomes a sacred link with God and others, a force for healing in a broken world. The notion of a God who is motion as well as love (love-in-motion), lightning as well as light (light-in-motion), gives me courage to face the emptiness, to meet chaos with creativity and originality, and (in a Godlike way) stretch out toward possibility. Then my own life becomes not only a work of art fashioned out of love, but a eucharistic process as well. The incarnation into a particular art form is the bodying forth of spiritual energy sacramentally into the perceptual world, and the bodying forth, the incarnation within the creative act, is always a Great Thanksgiving, an expression of deepest gratitude for creation itself.

My own gift to the collective theological process in the Christian community, and the gift of artists as a whole to the Church, is a sacramental attitude toward life. My way of creating theology—language and concepts and metaphors which describe my experience of God—is to perceive intrinsic unities and organic wholenesses in patterns of relationship at every level of experience. These patterns of unity and wholeness take the shape of infinite diversity of expression. The dynamics of their unfolding revelation of inner relatedness through outer forms are lively and omnipresent. My mind stretches almost to breaking when I learn from modern physics that everything in the universe participates in the incomprehensible movement of God: not only do we live as organically connected with the stars—our bodies and the oldest forms in the universe, the Giant Red Stars, containing the same substances of iron and calcium and phosphorous—but at the subatomic level endless processes relate substances in a continuous pattern of interchange and creation. I consider science and scholarship at their best to be forms of art, for art itself comes from the Latin, *artus, joint;* art is the creative *joining* of forms in order to create new forms. The scientists who tell me I am connected physically with the stars and the artists who create the cosmic dance and evoke the energy of miracles with color on canvas *both* open me to the sacramental dimension of life in which I perceive God moving and alive.

My very limited perception and understanding of astronomy spills over into poetry, the area of homage to the holy:

Universal Body

Worldflesh:
my bones bones
of the Old Red Stars.

And the little I am able to grasp of physics staggers my imagination, much less so than true physicists such as Capra are staggered, for their greater knowledge brings them to greater awe. I learn that physics today is not what it was when I first read about atomic structure in the seventh grade. Now scientists know that, while electrons fly in unimaginable circuits around the atomic nuclei at 600 miles per second, the nuclei themselves fly at 40,000 miles per second! Intense confinement creates intense velocity. And matter itself is nothing more than infinite varieties and interchanges of motion, so that physicists speak of matter's tendencies to occur rather than its absolute existence, and measure it by its possibilities. Everything consists of *possibility waves*. This fires my intuition even when my intellect is boggled, and teaches me more about God than a hundred catechisms. It also gets me more deeply in touch with what it means to be Godlike and human in an intricate and expanding universe. As Capra writes of the Tao of physics and calls it a way with a heart, he opens me to new levels of my own reality in the creature community:

> No such thing as empty space.
> No such thing as solid matter.
> No such thing as one time.

> > space is curved
> > matter is motion
> > here is possible
> > now is all

> The yellow canoe all by itself
> without being moved is moving itself
> faster than the white rapids around it.

> The red velvet couch I lie on
> moves a million times faster than my thoughts.
> My own body and yours moving so fast
> our faces cannot keep up.

> Which is why they—the faces—wrinkle first,
> in no-time, so the skin can get closer to itself.

These are perceptions and feelings and understandings of inexpressible realities. They are the processes which I bring to my own participation in theology-making as part of the Christian community. They are personal and experiential, intellectual and intuitive, sensual and bodily expressions of life from where I live it. At this moment, you are seeing my process only as it is for the instant. You are not aware of the changes I am undergoing even as I express my self in the present moment, for the act of expression changes my perception, just as communication is always determined by the

210

changing nature of the relationship in which it occurs. This happens so fast that I myself am not aware of it. At some point in the future I can look back to where I was, and in so doing, I can see that where I am now (where I shall be then) is a different place. And the change most often will have occurred without my knowing it. The gift of the past is in revealing the present to us through an awareness of our processes of change and growth. The unfolding discovery of these multi-level processes is what I mean by a "holistic" approach to theology—one which moves toward deeper wholeness through creative interplay of all available energies.

As theology is the descriptive, conceptual language of expressive, actual experience, it plays back into the experience by informing our worship. Liturgy is always created in a theological context, so that it is an accurate expression of the community's relationship to the holy. So-called "experimental" liturgies are the creative testing field of whole-making. A philosophy of theology that defines it as a whole-making (holistic) process also assumes that the *living* of theology in worship will be whole-making. Spirituality manifested collectively becomes liturgy. One of the members of our Wisdom House worshipping community recently created a Liturgy of Dreams, bringing that dimension of experience openly into our corporate act of worship.

In order to be part of such collective whole-making activities in the formation of theology and liturgy, it's necessary first to have trust in one's own processes. I have to be able to trust my experience in order to share it with others. I'm concerned with this more personal side of theology-making, and my concern has taken me into one more area of priestly ministry—that of therapy. Therapy—psychotherapy in this case—is for me the process of personal whole-making. Psychotherapy is the care of the soul, and aims toward the health of the soul as the person's total life center. As I bring creativity, poetry, dance, drama, and healing skills to the

211

therapeutic encounter, my purpose is to share a relationship which tends toward the healing and growth of each person involved in it. I have experienced the priestly ministry in therapeutic encounters with my clients, but I did not know until recently of the sacred origins of the art of therapy. Before the Greeks referred to healers as therapists, the word was used in naming those who functioned as interpreters for the Oracle at Delphi. Without therapists, sacred prophecy was useless, for no one could understand it. The therapists made wholeness between prophecy and the people, working as the prophet's priests to mediate deepest healing into the community.

My own personal process of whole-making has directly affected my spirituality and my contribution to my worshiping community. When our theological language was one-sidedly male, our liturgical language was also one-sidedly male. In fact, there are relatively few instances in which this is not still so. As I came to own and accept and celebrate my womanhood as a gift from God, bringing my own new value for the female side of life into prayer, my experience of God broke wide open. When I first began to use female imagery in prayer, I experienced a kind of inward leaping that was ecstatically physical as well as "spiritual," an inward bodily leaping that made me feel God in my nerves and blood and deep down in my bone marrow, as well as in my emotions and intellect.

As I grew in appreciation of the Hebrew and early Christian sources of reverence for the feminine in the divine, I laid deeper claim on my own God-experience as a woman reaching back to ancient collective female roots of worship. The mystical tradition in Jewish and Christian religion has always included the feminine aspect of God's nature, and I found validation for my own experience in Scriptures and in the saints. The Hebrew words for Spirit, Wisdom, and the Law, are all feminine words describing the feminine energy of

212

God. *Ruach,* the breath of the Spirit, expresses the creative energy of God, and the feminine *Shekinah* is God's abiding Presence, personified as the bride of Israel, as is the *Sabbath,* even as Israel is conversely called the bride of Yahweh, the masculine aspect of God. (See *The Hebrew Goddess,* by Raphael Patai, for discussion of the divine feminine in the spiritual history of Israel.) In the Christian tradition, Julian of Norwich spoke of her relationship with *Mother Jesus;* Anselm described a vision in which God appeared to him as a lactating woman who fed him heavenly food from her breasts; and the Patristic description of the Persons of the Trinity as male was compensated in an underlying experience of the Holy Spirit as the feminine energy identified with *Ruach,* and the life-giving Wisdom of *Hokmah* or *Sophia.* The virtual elevation and inclusion of Mary into the Trinity by the Roman Catholic concept of her as Co-redemptrix, and by the dogmas of the Immaculate Conception and Assumption, are spontaneous corrections for the patriarchal exclusion of the feminine in the official Christian theology of the nature of God.

Describing my own theological inclusiveness and spiritual expansiveness, in keeping with those tendencies in my own religious tradition, I wrote:

Mother Christ, Sister Spirit

Christ! Thank God you
are no longer the husband/lover
icon of my inner eye
(any more than you should be
for the soul's good eros),
nor the towering Master, lowering Lord
of my early childhood sleep,
but have at last risen
within my self's reality,
One-Who-Simply-Is.

213

Brother Jesus, Mother Christ,
creation's climax loving me through incarnation;
you stand by without/within,
heal, nurture, strengthen,
making me possible as you are possible.

Creator, Savior, Spirit,
beyond gender yet encompassing all:
Mother Bear to this wild cub,
Brother Lion to this lamb
(or Brother Lamb to this lion);
most wonderful of all, Sister Spirit
to this wakening woman, this human star.

On the collective side, I have served as liturgist for my own worshiping community, striving to redeem and reauthenticate liturgical language and imagery by making it conform with an inclusive theology of worship. In our Wisdom House Eucharistic liturgy, we speak of the Persons of the Trinity as Creator, Savior, and Sanctifier, emphasizing the aspects of God's activity rather than the one-sided sexual imagery devised by patriarchy. In the Creed, the transcendence of God is recognized in the First Person of the Creator, who is beyond gender; the immanent masculine is recognized in the human person of Jesus (though not necessarily in the eternal Christ, the Creative Word); and the immanent feminine is celebrated in the Holy Spirit, the Giver of life:

We believe in one God, Creator Almighty,
Maker of heaven and earth, of all that is seen and
    unseen.

We believe in one savior, Jesus Christ,
the firstborn of God, eternally given by the Maker.
Through Christ all things came to be.

For us and for our salvation Christ came from heaven:
by the power of the Holy Spirit he was born of the
Virgin Mary
and became human.
For our sake he was crucified under Pontius Pilate;
he suffered, died, and was buried.
On the third day he rose again in fulfillment of the
scriptures;
he ascended into heaven and is seated at the right
hand of the Maker.
He will come again in glory to judge the living and
the dead,
and his glory will have no end.

We believe in the Holy Spirit.
She is the giver of life who proceeds from the Maker;
with the Creator and the Savior
she is worshipped and glorified.
She has spoken through the prophets.

We believe in one holy catholic and apostolic Church.
We acknowledge one baptism for the forgiveness of
sins.
We look for the resurrection of the dead,
and the life of the world to come. Amen.

In the Eucharistic Prayer, we remember our forebears from
ancient times:

O God of our Mothers and Fathers,
God of Abraham and Sarah, Isaac and Rebecca;
God and Giver of Christ our Savior;
open our eyes to see your hand
at work in the world around us. . . .

We recognize that worship, like theology, is a living process subject to continuous evaluation and re-visioning. It's not a fixed object impervious to change, for liturgy and theology expand and contract in rhythm with the rest of our lives. Currently, liturgy and theology are expanding in some of our faith and worship communities, reflecting a life process of personal and co¹lective self-examination, expansion, and inclusion.

The value of inclusiveness and expansiveness in prayer, liturgical or devotional, public or private, is to help us get closer to God, to accurately express and enhance our present relationship to the holy. We do not presume to capture the reality of God in the language which describes our understanding of God, only to express our limited perception of our relationship with God at this moment in our religious lives. In this process, we discover that God is truly both immanent and transcendent, within and beyond, female and male, light and dark, merciful and just. The only model that I know of for the paradoxical, pararational self-revelation of God as we perceive it, is the apparently self-contradictory light theory in modern physics: light is manifested truly as waves, and truly as particles, alternately and at the same time, even though (we think) we know that waves and particles are irreconcilably different from one another in function. It isn't the light which is wrong, or the theory which is lacking, but our understanding which is limited, and our language which is always symbolic rather than exactly precise or directly descriptive. We are faced with an even greater mystery when we approach God. This is why it's never enough to approach God with anything less than our whole selves, all our functions working together: bodily, intellectually, emotionally, with the engagement of the whole organic self, experiencing and relating to the holy in life.

I was not able to approach God with this kind of engagement until I began to open up my prayer life to the feminine aspect of God, and to celebrate my own femaleness

216

in that aspect. And I didn't suspect the wholeness that I missed until I began to experience it. Then I came alive and knew that I wanted more and more *life* in my relationship with God and with other persons. From increased intimacy with God, my awe of God also increased, and so did my longing for authenticity in community, the longing of depth for depth.

I don't suggest that this process is possible only for women. I only know that I came to it self-consciously as a woman, open to deeper discovery of my own nature through closer contact with the nature of God and deeper contact with the nature of creation. Sexuality and spirituality interact in my own growth experience, and are reunited in my religious life.

My experience of feminine imagery in prayer begins to compensate for a personal life-time and several collective millennia of spiritual one-sidedness. Reclaiming the feminine in worship helps me to reclaim my self as a person created uniquely in the image of God, female. Now I know with my whole being that I am connected with God and with all creatures, organically and naturally, and that the realization of this connection is the reason for which I was born.

Slowly, steadily, I am learning, through constant refinement of feeling and thought, how to worship our Creator, how to wrap the world in prayer. The way is ancient, timeless, but I have to learn it each day for the first time. It is older than the earth, newer than the first leaf of spring.

Bakerwoman God

Bakerwoman God,
I am your living bread.
Strong, brown Bakerwoman God,
I am your low, soft, and being-shaped loaf.
I am your rising

bread, well-kneaded
by some divine and knotty
pair of knuckles,
by your warm earth hands.
I am bread well-kneaded.

Put me in fire, Bakerwoman God,
put me in your own bright fire.

I am warm, warm as you from fire.
I am white and gold, soft and hard,
brown and round.
I am so warm from fire.

Break me, Bakerwoman God!
I am broken under your caring Word.
Drop me in your special juice in pieces.
Drop me in your blood.
Drunken me in the great red flood.
Self-giving chalice, swallow me.
My skin shines in the divine wine.
My face is cup-covered and I drown.

I fall up
in a red pool
in a gold world
where your warm
sunskin hand is there
to catch and hold me.
Bakerwoman God, remake me.

Possibility

Limenality[1]

To live at the edge
I said,
I do not choose
but have been chosen
by the threshold.
Here.
I teeter,
stressed
beyond tensiveness,
a wild animal,

blackshining
she-lion
or she-bear.
Here.

The only way out is all the way in.

Young, dying
as surely as age,

---

[1] State of being at the threshold.

a ragged goat
or deer,
bloodblack hairs
standing on edge
all lightning charged.

Brinked.
Born out of fear.
The beast I am alive.

I teeter,
steerless
beyond sane,

a she-lion
or bear,

my body a quiver,
a furrowing roar,

trusting the terror.

Now in my dream I have just driven across a bridge. It is
starting to be night. There is a tremendous amount of
traffic—the rush hour. I am driving alone. The traffic forces
me to bear left after I cross the bridge. I am trying to remember the way home, and know that this is not it. I drive
down a winding, descending road until I come to lights and
people. I try to ask directions, but no one speaks my language. I try to phone my family, but there is no answer.
Finally one of the men at the gas station tells me in broken
English to drive back up the hill and turn left again when I
come to "Dark Street." Dark Street is a road that goes
straight up the side of a vertical cliff. It is impossible to drive

a car there. I decide he expects too much, and understands nothing. I get back in my car, drive back up the hill, go back to the bridge, and trust my own sense of direction for the ride home. I know that all my turns will be right this time, since there is no more traffic pushing me where I do not want to go.

In fast sequence with this dream I find myself in another one, this time in church at a Eucharist, where I am functioning as a deacon. (These dreams were before my ordination to the priesthood.) The priest who is presiding at the liturgy does not speak English. He consecrates Chinese egg rolls for Holy Communion. When it's time for us to give Communion to the worshippers, I see dismay in their eyes. The old women take the egg rolls with distressed resignation. The young women reject them, and plead with me to give them true Communion. I say that I don't know how I can, but I will try. I go after the male priest to ask him to consecrate bread, but he runs away and is gone. From somewhere (I do not know where), I find consecrated bread, and return to the women at the altar to feed it to them, as if by some miracle.

Through sometimes impossible, impenetrable obstacles, now and then losing my way, alone and with others, my life has been a relentless quest for wholeness and authenticity in the actualization of a calling I could not deny. My personal quest has taken place within the context of a community of faith. As I seek personal authenticity, I unite with others on similar quests, to form a community of pilgrims. Together we create and define our common authority. The word *authority* comes from the Greek words meaning "to achieve selfhood" (*autos* = self, + *hentes* = achieve). It is also connected with the Latin word, *augere*, "to increase." Genuine authority experienced in community enables each one in the community to act as a subject, not a passive object to be acted upon; it gives each one the power and integrity of an *author*, a creative self. From this creative self, personal authenticity is born, which feeds back into and strengthens the authority of the whole. Increase is experienced in personal wholeness and corporate integrity.

I've experienced this process in recent years as a boundary person, in the context of a boundary community on the edge of the institutional Church. Initially, many of us were pushed toward the edge by an institution which rejected our gifts, the very gifts it was in large part responsible for forming in us, for it was once the community in which we were centered, with which we identified.

As my dreams indicate, I have been forced to launch out on my own, trusting my own sense of direction in this process, but I have also never left the institutional community, though my relationship to it has changed. I have had to go outside it in search of sacred bread, but then, having found this bread as if by miracle beyond the Church, I've never lost sight that the bread was for the Church; I've brought it back into the Church to feed to the people there whom I serve. But the process has taught me that there are those outside the Church's walls who need and want the same living bread, the same cup of healing shared by those within. Because I had to go outside, beyond the walls to find the bread for myself and the community I served, my community expanded to include all those on the outside whose lives have touched mine in my own search for the true, the authentic bread of life.

Because I never left the institutional Church through this process, it's been forced to deal with me, to redefine itself in relationship to me, as I have had to redefine myself in relationship to it. We—the institutional Church and I—have helped each other to grow by standing with and against one another at the same time.

In the beginning of my interfacing with the institutional Church as a *womanpriest*, I was pushed toward its boundary, not by choice. While I still considered myself a faithful Episcopalian, others thought of me differently. I seemed neither in nor out of the institutional Church. I was living at that ambiguous place on the edge. It could have become a cutting edge, but from the beginning, part of my survival was to define that place as the growing edge, not only of the institution where I still had connections, but of my own life as well. During the public service of recognition of the priesthood of Jeannette Piccard and myself, a form was used which had been developed to admit Roman Catholic priests into the ecclesial structure of the Episcopal Church. I wondered out loud to a brother priest one day: "I'm being treated as if I have been outside the Episcopal Church. But if that's true, where have I been these three years?" He answered, "Why, you've been a priest in communion with the Apostolic Succession, beyond the Episcopal Church and floating freely in the historical process of continuity itself."

His words made me see life on the boundary in a different light. I grew sad to think of giving up the freedom of this place by accepting official status as a priest in the Episcopal Diocese of Minnesota. Then I realized that accepting recognition would give me more, not less freedom. Before, I was pushed toward the boundary; now I could choose it freely, embrace it with reverence, claim it ever more passionately as my home, a place which would become more than before *a place of possibility*—a place where I can come and go, alone and with others.

Now I perceive myself as a priest for the river people, the nomadic tribe of pilgrims who have settled by the river's edge on both sides of the institutional Church. The river people form a lively community of seers and shamans, those whose vision extends beyond themselves to include the larger meaning of God's quest for us and our quest for God. Ours is a parainstitutional but legitimate process, one which conforms with the functions of the prophetic community through the ages.

The people who live near the river of life often find themselves in the river, sometimes caught up in the breathtaking power of its independent movement, sometimes refreshed and renewed in its serenity. I frequently find myself in the river, enjoying its vitality. Here I am free to invite people from both sides to come into the river and join one another in its life-giving powers. The river becomes a place where bishops and feminists, professional women and homemakers, Roman Catholics and Unitarians, agnostics and evangelists, Marxists and capitalists, married, single, divorced, widowed, hetero- or homosexual, young and old can meet one another face to face without defenses, casting aside for the moment the fear of differences which has separated them. Then they may invite one another out of the river back up onto one shore or the other, learning to share their differences in mutual self-giving as equals, not to convert, but to care about and learn from each other. I remain free to claim the river itself for my home, and at the same time to move about on either shore with integrity, claiming a place for myself deep inside and far beyond the boundaries of the institutional Church. There is little security here, and considerable risk, but as I asked earlier, what is life without risks?

I continue to need connections with radical Christians in secular and religious communities, to need the solidarity of sisterhood with other feminists, to need to be accountable to other pilgrims on the way. I live where nothing can be taken for granted, or all will be lost.

Life on the edge means living creatively on the growing edge of my own life as well as on the growing edge of the institution. It means, sometimes in the face of strong opposition, finding a way not just to survive, but to live with abundance of life. Life on the edge is a stretching of the boundaries of our institutions, for we pull them with us as we expand ourselves. Life on the edge is full of the tension between the now and the not-yet, the real and the ideal, the present and future. The boundary community lives by faith experienced radically, at the roots, from the inside out, for faith, as Bultmann said, "is to be open to the genuine future."

Boundary theology requires that we move in the direction dictated by the challenges of growth, no matter the cost. In the words of the Dutch Catechism, "In a world of ascending evolution, sin is the refusal to grow in the direction which conscience dictates."

The boundary community is necessarily ecumenical, reaching for truth in all directions, seeking the holy in all available places and events, consecrating human experience from wherever life is genuinely lived. The day will come when what we are making of human community now will become the institution which future generations must move against in order to challenge and re-authenticate. Our hardest task is to build good and sturdy houses for our life together, yet houses that won't be a burden when we or our children judge that they must be left behind for newer, truer places later on.

What motivates us, and sometimes drives us, is the seed of original grace in each one of us, the recurring grace born anew in every child in every generation, manifested as a common desire for freedom, justice, community, and love. Though its perpetual destruction gives us pain, its perpetual resurgence is the source of our deepest faith.

My model for boundary theology is the non-structured style of the New Testament communities, where gifts and needs were recognized and mutually fulfilled, and where internal tensions were worked out with courage and mutual commitment to the personal and collective good. I choose this life by the river, for I believe that all people are God's people (though some may choose to disclaim their birthright as God's children). I find the whole of humanity too enriching to cut myself off from any aspect of it which can lead me closer to God, to my own truth, and to our shared understanding of what life on earth means. I live by the river as a resurrection priest, to an extent unrecognizable, yet truly risen with Christ, truly new, truly in communion with others. These are the values of the river of life for me as a Christian priest, and as a human person.

In summary, I close with a description of my calling that I was asked to write for the *Bulletin* of St. Joan's International Alliance, U.S. Section:

I never know where to begin when someone asks me how I came to the priesthood. Sometimes I feel that I was born for it; sometimes it seems the strangest accident. Both of these must be true. I came to it organically and mysteriously (*mysterium tremendens*).

Organically: I was chrismated (baptized/confirmed) Russian Orthodox—my mother's tradition—when I was six months old. When I was three, my father became an Episcopal deacon and priest. I grew up perceiving ministry as completely normal. It all came naturally! I participated in the ministries of both my parents ever since—and before—I can remember. In my early teens I experienced the beginnings of a definite call to religious life. But a vocation to ministry and to a sacramental life came much earlier; it grew with me from my earliest awareness. I knew the liturgy by heart. For me, the sacraments were as much the fibre of my life as food and air. When I was old enough the sacramentality of human relationships became a cherished ministry in itself: truly being with and living for others. This, after all, is the essence of the priestly life, a life of sacrifice, of making holy or of re-cognizing the holy everywhere, pointing to it for others, and celebrating it with others. When I was eighteen I began to make poems and publish them seriously. It was finally this call to poetry that made me sure of my own priesthood in the human community, in Christ's community. The sacramental act of making words into flesh drew me deeper into the incarnational mystery and reality of Christ alive in our midst.

Mysteriously: It was impossible. A poet? All right. A religious? Yes, fine: cheap laborer in the vineyard. But a woman and a priest? Never! Heresy! Anathema! Oh? First, I aimed for the diaconate, the pastoral ministry of the Church which was open to women. It is all right for women to be deacons because deacons are caring servants. But priests are leaders! They guard the sacred mysteries! Women would contaminate the purity of these mysteries and of the faith! How does any of this fit in with the Gospel? It is *anti-Gospel*. So the double message I heard from the Church: "You are a child of God, heir of the freedom of the children of God," and "You are a woman and less than human; you can never re-present Christ to others; you are worthy of baptism but not of priesthood." Enough to make one begin to ask some serious questions, yes? I began asking and I am still asking. And asking has led me to frightening things: to prophecy, to priesthood itself, to surprise by joy, to moments of terrible loneliness and fear; but it has also led me deeper into the heart of God, into the arms of the Christian community, into integrity and clearer faith, into the holy reality of sisterhood, into the warmth of my sisters' and brothers' radiant love and acceptance, and into new life with others.

Now the future: I cannot even imagine it. My values have changed over the last two years. I value

227

freedom over security, community over institution, creativity over order. My self-definition has changed. Being a priest isn't being set over a community, it's being set at the heart of the community, an alive and active symbol of the priesthood of a holy people. The most significant thing about my priesthood is that it's a symbol of your priesthood. I live to be a symbol for you; if you look at me and see the icon of Christ-in-you, then my ministry is worth something. Otherwise, it's mere ecclesiastical foolishness. I hope to go on doing what I've been doing: discovering, defining, creating my own life, my own reality, my own priestly ministry in struggle and joy, alone and with others, claiming my selfhood in the image of God, affirming my sisters as icons of Christ as much as my brothers. I do this in the ambience of my religious community, Ecumenical Oblates, where we place ourselves under the guidance of Holy Wisdom, under her healing wings at Wisdom House in Minneapolis. I do this with a man who is not only my lover, but my brother, in a marriage where we are priests for each other. I do this in working to make myself as independent as possible from institutions, personally and professionally, in my ministry of psychotherapy. I do this by living out feminism as I see it lived by Jesus and the women in the gospels. I do it as a poet, a creator, like you, like every human being. ... Last night I fell asleep with T. S. Eliot's words in my body:

We shall not cease from exploration
and the end of all our exploring
will be to arrive where we started
and know the place for the first time.

228

And a traditional Japanese haiku:

> I have always known
> that at last I would take this road
> but yesterday I did not know
> that it would be today.

My search goes on. I wish you well in yours.